Advance Praise for
The Spare Room

"Filled with positivity in the midst of a changing, complex world, this book weaves a narrative of inspiring stories and practical advice. *The Spare Room* is a lighthouse in today's storm...a call to action for anyone seeking to live a more intentional, purposeful life."

—**Arianna Huffington,** Founder and CEO, Thrive Global

"Emily Chang understands the power of the magic wand each one of us has when we pay attention to other people's feelings, and her wonderful book, *The Spare Room,* is a testimony of that! A must read to open our hearts!"

—**Diane von Furstenberg**

"In today's business world, social purpose has become an urgent leadership imperative. Emily Chang exemplifies values-based leadership and has committed her life to improving those around her, both at work and in her community. For anyone seeking to lead with authenticity and purpose, *The Spare Room* provides a step-by-step manual to defining your own brand of leadership."

—**Robert A. McDonald,** 8th Secretary of the Department of Veterans Affairs,
Retired Chairman, President and CEO of The Procter & Gamble Company

"Emily Chang boldly swings open the door to her family's life stories, welcoming us into her private world in order to shine a public light on today's need for socially purposeful leaders with hearts of hospitality."

—**Horst Schulze,** Cofounder of Ritz-Carlton and Author of *Excellence Wins*

"A book every leader must read, *The Spare Room* is the ultimate playbook for those who want to lead and live with intention. Alongside poignant stories from her own life and those of other professionals across a wide spectrum of industries, Emily Chang is an inspiration!"

—**Laura Alber,** CEO, Williams-Sonoma

"This book is a must read for anyone looking to lead a life of intention and social purpose. Drawing from her own firsthand experiences and those of others, Emily offers inspiring stories that are sure to leave readers asking themselves how they can help make a difference by sharing their own 'spare rooms' with those in need."

—**Stephanie Fischer,** President and CEO, Global Retail Marketing Association

"Emily Chang leads from a higher calling. As a global CEO, she leads with extreme talent and a deep desire to love her neighbor as herself, positively impacting everyone she meets. *The Spare Room* is a delightful narrative of moving testimonies—taking you on a journey from heart to mind to impact. It is a deep well from which comes the pure waters of living and leading with intention!"

—**Rick Lytle,** President and CEO of CEO Forum

"I believe God creates each of us with purposes far greater than we can imagine. *The Spare Room* is a personal guide to discovering your God-given passion and resources so you can do more with the one life you've been given. My friend Emily Chang offers a compelling call to a more purposeful journey, anchored in her own life experiences and backed by a constructive framework and practical tools. Read this book to uncover your unique way to make a difference in the world by living into your social legacy."

—**Edgar Sandoval Sr.,** President, World Vision U.S.

"The most immediately actionable book I've read in a while! Chock-full of interesting, heartwarming stories, followed by a thoughtful tool kit so that, regardless of where you are in life, you can begin living with more purpose and intention. Highly recommend this beautiful collection of poignant stories."

—**Yarrow Kraner,** CEO, HATCH

"Emily Chang's life philosophy is an incredibly authentic display of emotional intelligence and business ingenuity. Her creativity and wisdom shine through every page of *The Spare Room*, which serves as the quintessential blueprint for any established or aspiring leader building a heart-first organization. Having led world-class companies through the ever-shifting tides of culture, it's no surprise that her expertise lends itself perfectly to the growing global need for social-ly-driven leaders and companies. Also, she's got the coolest hair you'll ever see."

—**Chris Denson,** Award-Winning Innovation Advocate and Book Author, Host of *Innovation Crush*

THE
SPARE
ROOM

THE
SPARE
ROOM

Define Your Social Legacy
to Live a More Intentional Life
and Lead with Authentic Purpose

EMILY CHANG

Post Hill
PRESS

A POST HILL PRESS BOOK

The Spare Room:
Define Your Social Legacy to Live a More Intentional Life and Lead with
Authentic Purpose
© 2021 by Emily Chang
All Rights Reserved

ISBN: 978-1-64293-762-6
ISBN (eBook): 978-1-64293-763-3

This is a work of nonfiction. All people, locations, events, and situations are portrayed to the best of the author's memory.

Cover design by Abraham Cano
Interior design and composition by Greg Johnson, Textbook Perfect

Post Hill Press
New York • Nashville
posthillpress.com

Published in the United States of America
1 2 3 4 5 6 7 8 9 10

To Minki, for being our rock, grinding fresh coffee each morning, and dancing like an electrocuted robot.
You're why there's good *kibun* in our home.

To Laini, the coolest person I know, who crafts stunning jewelry, fills our home with soulful cello music, and makes me laugh till I'm incapacitated. You give me joy.

To each occupant of our spare room. We love you.

Contents

Author's Note

While I have personally interviewed the people whose stories are in this book and have carefully documented most of their stories, I had the privilege of hearing Marlene's, Josie's, and Thomas's stories in passing and, as a result, have done my best to reflect the experiences they shared in one-time sittings. I have changed the names and identifying characteristics of Lia, Devon, and Lotus to protect them from recognition. Dialogue has occasionally been approximated, and I have shared my own stories (the first in each chapter) the best that my family and I remember them.

Preface

I n 2011, I was offered an exciting executive position, leading retail marketing for Apple across the Asia Pacific. Upon accepting the offer, my partner of eleven years and three-year-old daughter relocated with me from the U.S. to Shanghai, China. This move opened a new, exhilarating chapter in our personal and professional lives. At work, I was learning every day and loving every minute of my job. Life was full and richly rewarding, and in truth, we didn't realize that anything was missing until we met Teo.

At just eighteen months old, Teo was still the size of a newborn and, more important, he was dying. He had been born with extreme hydrocephalus and a head so distended with fluid that his eyelids were unable to close. And by the time we met him, the unblinking, unresponsive baby had already endured unspeakable pain and tragedy. After suffering through a barbaric surgery conducted by a fraudulent doctor, the badly injured baby was left with an orphanage by parents who had given up all hope. Eventually, a nonprofit organization discovered him in the corner of the facility and reached out to us, convinced we were the right family to care for him.

The little boy's situation seemed overwhelming, and we initially declined, not feeling equipped for the task. "She's too young to see something like this, right?" I asked my husband, referring to our daughter. An enormously compassionate man, Minki paused before responding.

"Actually, I think she understands enough about death to grasp the situation, but I'm concerned about her having to witness that degree of pain."

We were still busy convincing each other to decline when my four-year-old overheard us and gave us a good talking-to.

"Mom, what's that baby you talking 'bout?" little Laini demanded as she rounded the corner.

We explained to her about the baby boy, emphasizing his serious medical condition. I wrapped up with, "Babe, I'm worried it's too much for you, maybe too much for us."

But my daughter lifted a tiny resolute finger and demanded with her cute lisp, "Mom, we *have* to get him! You said we should always help if we can. That's what we *do*! We take care of kids who need a *home*. So, let's go get him...*right now*!" That day, Laini not only touched us with her simple, generous spirit, but she also galvanized us around our family's social purpose. We had indeed agreed that our spare room would always be open to vulnerable young people who needed a safe place to live. This was the social legacy we sought to leave behind in each of our communities, and Laini had reminded us that it was, in fact, exactly what Teo needed.

Bringing Teo home served as an inflection point for our family. Though his situation had seemed overwhelming, we found that we always have capacity to invest in our social legacy and that our lives become incredibly enriched when we lean into that commitment.

I also realized that being intentional in my personal purpose made me a more effective leader at work. Caring for a special-needs child at home helped me approach my job in a more empathetic manner. And particularly working in a people-oriented service industry, I realized the way I lived my life enabled my teams to see me as an authentic servant leader. This helped develop trust, dissolve rigid layers of corporate hierarchy, and enable deeper personal relationships. Then, much to our delight and beyond our wildest imaginations, Teo not only survived but lived with us for years, bringing laughter, love, and indescribable joy to our home.

Teo was the twelfth occupant of our spare room. Over the course of the past twenty-one years, we have welcomed sixteen children and young people into our home. Life has regularly served up those in need, sometimes directly to our doorstep. And each time the door to our spare room has opened, I have found myself in a front-row seat, witnessing one of life's incredible stories unfold.

That's why our family has come to see our ability to help those who need a safe place to stay as our life's purpose and social legacy. I believe that when we find the intersection of that injustice that deeply offends us and what it is we have to offer, we narrow in on our unique opportunity to have an impact and make a meaningful contribution.

We all experience that visceral response to something that offends our sense of justice, the thing that makes us stop in our tracks, thinking: "This cannot go on. Someone has to do something!" I call this the Offense. Similarly, we each have something we're uniquely positioned to offer. That Offer is a resource we have on hand, which may sit idly by while another person desperately needs just that thing. It's when Offer and Offense come together that social legacy is born.

For my family, sharing our spare room has literally cost us nothing. It otherwise sits empty and furnished, littered only with a few dusty books and an unused yoga mat. And while not everyone may feel comfortable inviting a stranger into their home, everyone does possess an unused resource or capability.

And you know what? There's someone out there in need of exactly your Offer.

Today, social purpose has also become an urgent leadership imperative in the business world. To be successful, each of us, regardless of industry or functional expertise, must lead with authenticity and purpose. And in order to embody social purpose and embed its values in the workplace, we must get clear on our own personal purpose. After all, it's tough to lead a socially responsible business if we aren't socially purposeful leaders.

If we reflect on those leaders who have most successfully inspired followership, we will realize that they are the ones who have been driven by something personally relevant and meaningful. Their convictions extend beyond thoughts, to action both in and out of work. For those of you who seek to articulate this sort of personal mission as a leader, I hope *The Spare Room* will provide a framework with which to determine your own social legacy. In this book, I will share my experiences over the past couple of decades, as well as other stories from a variety of inspiring leaders I've met. I will also provide practical exercises for personal reflection so that by the time you close this book, you will have identified your own social legacy and outlined an action plan.

Thank you for your interest in this book, and I hope with all my heart that you find the investment to be uplifting and life-enhancing.

CHAPTER 1

A Perfect Fit

What you have to offer
is exactly what someone else needs.

"The meaning of life is to find your gift.
The purpose of life is to give it away."

— PABLO PICASSO —

The Spare Room
New York, 1996

She was the daughter of Asian American immigrants, and Lia played her role of obedient Korean girl extremely well. Growing up in a middle-class suburban neighborhood, she knew exactly what was expected of her. She fastened her long, straight hair back tidily. She waited patiently at the dinner table, allowing her little brother to select the best morsels first. She practiced her violin every afternoon, studied hard, and brought home perfect grades.

Lia reveled in the moment her father would hold her test results between his two veiny hands. Spectacles sliding halfway down his pockmarked nose, chin jutting slightly forward, he held his head still as his eyes slowly scanned their way down

1

the paper. When they had traveled back up to the red A at the top of the page, he would give the slightest nod, handing the paper back to Lia without a word. This was what she worked so hard for, and his approval meant everything to her. The girl would feel her heart skip a beat as she demurely reclaimed her test. Then, when she had returned to her room, Lia would allow herself three long minutes of silent celebration. Lying with eyes closed on the pink floral comforter she'd long outgrown, she would breathe deeply and allow a glowing smile to slowly cross her face.

Her home was one of quiet concentration, studied discipline, and unsaid words. Lia's parents were both employed, so before they got home, it was up to her to complete all her schoolwork before dinner. She had to look after her brother, too, making sure he finished his homework. And while there was much to do, Lia relished those afternoons. Those cherished hours when she and her brother could casually chat at the table. The few unguarded moments before masks were slipped carefully back in place when her parents returned home.

Eomma and Appa arrived home between five and six o'clock every evening, grunting with satisfaction to find both children sitting at the glossy kitchen table, legs swinging softly as they noiselessly completed their studies. In the Lin household, family dinner conversation was tempered, as the children deferentially answered questions about their teachers and homework. Grateful that the clicking of chopsticks and the gentle slurping of seaweed soup effectively absorbed lulls in conversation, the children ate with concentration and downcast eyes.

Many years earlier, Lia had learned that her parents weren't like the parents of her American friends, who celebrated good grades with rowdy trips to Dairy Queen. Those sweet-smelling mothers who wore cashmere cardigans and pearls. Who hugged their daughters when they came home from school and cheered from the sidelines during school tennis tournaments. Those fathers who loosened their ties and rolled up their shirtsleeves, kicking back with a cold beer after work. American parents brought out chilled Jell-O molds after a dinner crammed with loud conversation and raucous laughter, and sometimes headed outside after the meal to kick a ball around with the kids before bedtime. Lia absolutely loved going over to her friends' houses for dinner. It was like stepping into a different universe. But as she sat at their love-worn wooden tables, whose veneer was so unlike the dark, polished one in her own home, she was often filled with a deep yearning. The sharp pang of envy was inevitably followed by a profound sense of guilt. Sometimes she had to pretend to go to the bathroom, just so she could sit on a closed toilet lid and wait for her head to stop spinning.

At school, Lia had learned to tuck her Banana Republic T-shirt in just so. She stuffed both corners casually into the front pockets, while the back hung sloppily over her jeans. She slung her backpack over her right shoulder, just like the other kids did. And she popped her gum just loudly enough to come across as coolly nonchalant, but not so loudly as to be annoying or seen as trying too hard. She floated through the school hallways, not fitting into any one particular clique. Lia was quietly sweet to everyone she met and carried her weight on the tennis team.

But the teenager didn't have much of a social life. After their first few invitations to parties had been rejected, the others had simply stopped inviting her. There was something about her parents' being really strict and not allowing her to go out on Friday nights, because she had Korean school on Saturday mornings. She couldn't go out on Saturday nights either, because she had to be at her Kumon math class by eight a.m. on Sunday, followed by swim class, and violin lessons after that.

There was also something a little weird about Lia. It made those around her feel the slightest bit uneasy. They couldn't quite put their finger on it.

To her peers, Lia seemed like a holograph. She could give the illusion of flickering between two different people at the same time. From one angle, $3.99 drugstore eyeliner and frosted lip gloss peeked through the long tresses of a typical teenage girl. From another, tears threatened to spill from fearful, anxious eyes, and her lips pressed tightly together, pale with anxiety. Somehow, Lia had an instinctual understanding that her classmates simply wouldn't understand her family, so she persevered in keeping her two worlds separate.

To her tennis team, Lia seemed like a racket strung a little too tightly. She seemed to love playing the game and enjoyed spending time with the team. Her power serve was something awesome to behold, particularly for such a small girl. But she played with a ferocity that bordered on intimidating. Like her oversized racket, Lia seemed stretched rigidly to maximum power but threatened to pop at any moment.

To the faculty, she should have been the dream student: quiet, studious, and respectful. But her teachers observed Lia with a reservation that bordered on unease. The girl awaited her grades with such apprehension, the teachers felt as though they had been granted a dreadful sort of power: the ability to deliver rapturous joy or incalculable suffering with the simple stroke of a red pen.

— · —

Have you ever seen that line where dry pavement ends and rain begins? On one side, the ground is dry and the sun is shining. But take one step more, and you need a raincoat and an umbrella. Or, have you experienced the reverse? One moment, you're driving through pouring rain, the wipers swiping frenetically across the windshield. Suddenly, you cross that line into sunny weather and rush to turn off the wipers as they squeak in protest.

This is what I think Lia must have felt like growing up. The girl struggled constantly to straddle two worlds: a coldly disciplined Korean household and the cheerful affections of American living. She oscillated between wanting to live the ordinary life of an American teenager and desperately wanting to please her Asian parents. And Lia's happiness was singularly determined by either her parents' silent nod of affirmation or the tempestuous fury that was unleashed when she failed to meet their expectations.

This was the Asian way. Perfect grades, unblemished musical performances, polite small talk with parents' friends... these defined the conduct of a good Korean daughter. Performing and behaving as expected invites no praise. But come home with an A- or allow stiff fingers to stumble over a complex Tchaikovsky run—these reflect cataclysmic failure. They represent not only the child's failure but the parents' as well. At this point, the child is not reprimanded or even spanked. Her privileges are not revoked. Rather, she is methodically and ruthlessly ground into emotional nothingness.

She is told she is worthless, that she has wasted her parents' hard-earned money. She will never amount to anything, and she has disgraced the family. See how her cousin is so much more successful? How lucky her aunt and uncle are to have such an obedient child! Such a *good* child! The girl's parents will bemoan their bad luck, having invested their hard-earned money in such useless offspring. They will tear at their hair and wonder aloud at what they must have done wrong in a former life to deserve such a useless girl.

This is just what happened the day Lia came home with a B- on her earth science test. She tremulously handed the paper to her father and watched as his face turned tomato red, then magenta, then a deep, terrifying purple. The man had simply stopped breathing, as the paper began to vibrate with the tremor of his rigid hands. Lia's mom drifted over from the kitchen and casually placed a hand on her husband's tense shoulder. As her eyes registered the big red markings on the page, her fingers started to tighten. Within seconds, they turned a startling white as they clenched his shoulder, the shirt fabric bunching submissively beneath dry, rough fingertips. Lia's anxiety skyrocketed. She felt as if those fingers were squeezing the very breath from her lungs. Then, the verbal assault began. She stood stoically as her parents lashed unrelentingly at her, tears rolling steadily down her face. Frustration and helplessness coursed through her, as the fateful words were unleashed: "After fourteen years, you still cannot bring home a good grade! You have made us *miserable*. You are *wretched*. You should just *leave* this house!"

Many Asian kids grow up hearing these kinds of words. To the ears of non-Asian Americans, they may sound terribly abusive. But most Asian American kids know deep inside that their parents don't hate them or think they're worthless. Rather, as immigrants, the parents have done everything to give their children a better life. They have left their homes and families to provide their children with more opportunities, pinning 100 percent of their lonely hopes on the next generation. That's why a child's every shortcoming is taken as a personal reflection of the parents' worth and it's no wonder the pressure threatens to boil over at any minute.

But for Lia that day, those words clawed mercilessly at her self-worth. She believed she had caused all her parents' misery. Her little brother never seemed to cause such drama; he always brought home good grades, and they adored him. She began to think that the family truly would be better off without her. A desperate hopelessness washed over her and so, without a destination in mind, Lia threw her journal, a toothbrush, and a change of clothes into her school backpack and shrugged it on over her zip-up windbreaker. She hurried out of the house, head down, sobbing inconsolably.

Over the next few days, Lia stayed at a friend's house. During the day while school was in session, she flipped through beauty magazines found under the dusty bed frame. Holding her darkest thoughts at bay, the teenager filled her head with celebrity gossip and fashion tips. At night, the girls would talk, and Lia would help her friend with homework assignments. But soon, her friend realized she couldn't keep hiding Lia in her room and sneaking food up at night. Besides, it seemed her parents were already onto her, and the girls worried that they would call Lia's family. So, she headed out on her own once again.

At this point, the girl's profound sadness had hardened into a cold, rebellious rage. Her parents' words had burrowed deep into her heart. Recklessly, she dove headfirst into every dangerous situation she came across. She soon lost her virginity in the dark, musty closet of a fraternity, to a pudgy sophomore whose moist flannel shirt reeked of stale beer. As he drunkenly shoved himself into her from behind, she caustically thought, "Why not now? If not him, it'll be some other boy. I might as well get it over with." Lia ended up staying in his dirty frat room for a few more weeks. She showered when the guys were in class, tidied up during the day, and tried to fit in with the college kids at night. One evening over a dinner of cold leftover pizza, she teasingly asked him if he thought she was mature for a fourteen-year-old kid, and the panicked boy threw her out. He'd had no idea how old she was.

This time Lia hit the streets, emboldened. Armed with the knowledge of her sexuality but unaware of her precious worth, she quickly fell in with the wrong crowd. Boys with too much hair gel and too much swagger followed her around. Men with straggly hair and sour breath brought her little gifts of stolen makeup and hand-rolled joints.

She chewed her black, ragged nails, ripped at her black, ragged jeans, and kicked at the curb with her black, scuffed Doc Martens. One night, she took apart a plastic BIC pen. Flashlight held tightly between gritted teeth, Lia gave herself an angry, jagged tattoo on the soft flesh of her inner arm that read "die slut." A few short weeks later, she learned how to steal Cheetos, beef jerky, and beer from the local 7-Eleven. Then Lia started sleeping around, trading sexual favors for food, shelter, and cigarettes.

It all led up to that last fateful night. She was lucky he only beat her up. It could have been so much worse. But there was still some self-preservation left in that hard little body, and she chose to run. Leaving her backpack behind with all her belongings, Lia fled as fast as she could down the stairs and into the streets. Too scared to turn and see if he was chasing her, the girl kept running until she tripped over a bump in the sidewalk, and sprawled face-first into a puddle of dirty rainwater. Bruised and trembling, Lia was still pulling herself together on the curb that dark, rainy night when my old Ford Tempo pulled up beside her.

— . —

That autumn, 1996, I was living alone in a small studio apartment and just starting my junior year at the University of Rochester. I was working full-time to pay for my tuition, car, and apartment, and completing each day's schedule required expert navigation of commuter traffic and a good dose of luck. Balancing classes, a prestigious Teacher's Assistant role, and off-campus work left me drained at the end of each long day.

One cold evening after a particularly grueling day, I sat impatiently at an intersection, yearning to get home and climb into bed with a bowl of steaming-hot soup. But having traveled this road every day for years, I sighed deeply, knowing this particular traffic light was an unreasonably long one. I glanced out the car window, and a bedraggled person caught my eye. In an all-too-familiar movement, I quickly locked the doors and trained my eyes back toward the light. But then, I slowly turned and looked again. This person was no threat to me. In fact, she was just a kid! As the light changed to green in the reflection of my watery dash, horns honked angrily and cars began to swerve indignantly around me.

And still I sat, torn with indecision. "I've got to get home. It's after eight, and I haven't even started that lab," I thought. As my heart clenched painfully for the shivering girl, my head retorted, "What would you do, anyway? You can barely pay your own rent!" But my conscience won out in the end. The idea of leaving behind this girl, who had obviously been injured, twisted indignantly in my stomach.

So, I unrolled my window and shouted out into the rain, "Hey, are you OK?" She slowly lifted her head at the sound of my voice. One eye already beginning to swell, she spat through bloody lips messily smeared with lipstick, "Fuck you!"

My inner voice declared, somewhat self-righteously, "There you go; you tried. Now step on the gas and get yourself home." But the light had turned red again. So, as I sat through another long wait, I invited the girl to dinner. There was a diner just down the street, and anyway, I had to eat, right? As she glared suspiciously at me, I promised, "No strings. Just a quick meal. Look, I just finished teaching an extra class tonight and have a few extra bucks to burn."

As the soaking-wet girl threw herself into my back seat, my car immediately filled with a dank, musty odor. Nose wrinkling, I realized that my old fabric seats were never going to smell the same again. But she was already firmly ensconced in the car, so I drove us to the diner, where we shared a greasy meal in silence. The girl dripped gray water into a slowly widening puddle on the floor, while I looked around uneasily, exchanging meaningful looks with our server. I'm ashamed to admit, I couldn't wait for the uncomfortable meal to end. When the food had disappeared from our plates, my dining companion peeled her jeans off the plastic seat and, without a word, began to walk away. My emotions swung rapidly from relief to guilt to uncertainty. Where was she going to sleep? It was freezing outside. The words flew out of my mouth before I had time to think: "Where are you going to stay? I've got a spare room."

Thirty minutes later, she glanced around my studio apartment and sardonically commented, "Spare room? *Pffft!* You ain't got no spare room. You only *got* one room. Where'm I supposed to sleep?" The small, intense girl was right. I lived in a tiny space, in what used to be the maid's quarters of an old mansion. But a girl with nothing didn't need much. Within an hour, she had showered in my tiny bathroom, borrowed some clothes, and fallen into a deep sleep on my old mustard-yellow couch.

When she first moved in, Lia treated me like a convicted pedophile. She glared distrustfully at me from a distance, positioning herself as far away as she could. She carried her food—which, on my budget, varied between macaroni and cheese and spaghetti with Ragú sauce—to the other side of the room to eat. Staring at each other from across the room, we shared meals of zero nutritional value in cold, unwavering silence.

Eventually, we fell into a sort of rhythm. I'd come home from work and begin making one of our starchy, sodium-laden meals. I chattered endlessly as the water bubbled. About how much I loved biology. About how I had a crush on my physics Teacher's Assistant. And how I was worried that my sputtering car was on its last legs. Though she didn't reply or ask questions, I could tell Lia was listening. So, I persisted with my evening monologues. By the third week, Lia began to sit the tiniest bit closer to me. After a month, she began listening with an expression that might have bordered on interest.

Then one day, I returned from class to find Lia gone. The paper envelope of cash I kept in a tin coffee can by the fridge was empty. I felt my heart drop heavily into my stomach and thought, "I hope no one robs her. I hope she knows enough to keep the cash hidden."

I can't say I was shocked, though I was surprised at the disappointment that washed over me. Since that first evening six weeks prior, I hadn't regretted inviting the young girl into my apartment. I didn't have much, but we had both soon realized that what I had to offer was just what she needed. And whether she admitted it or not, I knew Lia needed me. But now, she was gone.

Slowly pulling out my heavy organic chemistry books, I got to work with a deep sigh. And I hadn't realized I had dozed off until the sound of a key turning in the lock jolted me awake. Without a word, Lia walked in, balancing two heavy plastic bags. She didn't look at me, and she didn't say a word. She just started unpacking those iconic blue boxes of macaroni and cheese, four twenty-five-cent boxes of linguini, and two jars of Ragú sauce. My little roommate placed a carton of private-label milk in the fridge and carelessly dropped some change into the coffee can. Unable to contain the enormous smile stretching across my face, I thanked her. As my heart lifted, I thought: "Maybe people *do* rise to your highest expectations." I believe that was the moment in my life when I decided to choose optimism and hope over cynicism. Meanwhile, the girl responded to my joy with something between an exasperated huff and an amused sigh, then turned her back and flopped onto the couch.

Over the next few months, I discovered an affectionate, funny person in my roommate. She insisted on carrying her weight, and regularly did our grocery shopping. Lia kept the place clean and became increasingly interested in what I was studying. Sometimes, the fourteen-year-old girl would come sit on my lap and cuddle as I studied my textbooks. Occasionally, she would braid my long hair as I prepared for work. And late at night, I was occasionally gifted with heart-breaking glimpses of her time on the streets. Lying on the couch in the dark just a few feet away from my mattress on the floor (I had never bothered with a bed frame), Lia would unexpectedly open up and share a deeply personal memory. The next morning, she'd angrily push me away and not speak again for days. I tried to sense her moods, and adjusted to give her space. Over time, I learned when to ask questions and when to listen quietly. Eventually, we became friends...or sisters. We became something that doesn't really have a name. It was intensely special.

That same year, I began dating someone new, and I was worried about how he'd feel that I had a young girl living with me. But he was not only OK with it; this guy encouraged me to do what I could to help Lia. In fact, one night he showed me just how much he meant it.

We were studying for finals together, a stressful week for two science students on scholarship. Around eleven p.m., the phone rang—a jarring interruption that penetrated the stillness of our weary study session. A tearful Lia sobbed loudly into the phone and asked me to pick her up. It was a freezing-cold night, and she needed a ride home from the red-light district.

Before I could respond, my boyfriend stood up and shrugged on his jacket. He passed me a pen and notepad to write down where she was as he patted his pockets, searching for car keys. Gazing at him with newfound appreciation and love, I suddenly knew I'd marry this quiet, generous man. We've now been married for twenty years, and together we have shared our spare room with sixteen people.

I never did find out what had brought Lia to the red-light district that night, but life continued on in relative peace. Yet, while we'd settled into a comfortable rhythm and I could feel her pulling out of her shell, I also began to wonder about the future. This smart, thoughtful girl should be in school. Maybe she should return home. Though they'd said some terrible things, I was sure her parents would want to know she was safe. Yet whenever I brought up the subject, she shut me down. Hard. Dishes would shatter in the sink; doors would slam. And that dreaded but familiar silent treatment would descend once again upon the apartment.

— • —

One day, I approached a university Counselor and asked for advice about how to get Lia enrolled into a nearby high school. It turned out that I wasn't able to enroll her in the public school near my apartment, since I wasn't her legal guardian. Not surprisingly, I was strongly encouraged to return her to her family. Yet, Lia adamantly refused to go. Eventually, we found a way for her to live with a foster family and attend public school in a nearby district.

After she moved out, we kept in touch sporadically. Those were the days of pagers and voicemail. So, living on two different schedules and missing our late-night chats under the safe cover of darkness, Lia and I spoke less frequently. But she seemed to do all right with her foster family. I don't think Lia ever did contact her own family again...and I learned a valuable life lesson from this: words are insanely powerful. They're so much more powerful than we give them credit for, particularly as parents.

They burrow themselves into the heart, and the poisonous ones etch deeply into the soul. Thanks to Lia, I learned early on that we must be so, so careful about what we say. Especially to young people. We must know that our words will resound and echo. Maybe validating and building confidence. Maybe providing reassurance of unconditional love. Or maybe pushing the person into darkness or far, far away from us.

Another startling realization struck me only after Lia moved out. I looked back over the previous months and realized that I had shared life for a full semester in this small apartment with a young girl I hadn't even known. I caught a glimpse not just of the impact I could leave on those around me, but also of the real depth of our capacity to give. One dinner at a cheap local diner turned into one night in my apartment. Which rolled into another night, then a few weeks, and then a few months. I would never have thought I had the time or space for a teenage runaway in my studio apartment and with my busy schedule back then. But it turns out that our capacity to give far exceeds our wildest imagination. And as that giving unfolds, we realize just how much we have to offer. Lia showed me how the little I had was exactly what she needed.

If a harried college kid had it then, we must all have it in us, here and now. We just need to identify what we have to offer and extend it against an Offense that cannot be ignored. When we do this, we find ourselves at the center of our social legacy.

Twenty years later, I still vividly remember what Lia looked like, huddled in fear and pain on the side of the street. I remember the brittle, bitter edge of her suspicion, and I remember the childlike joy that occasionally bloomed late in the evening.

As the first kid to have shared my spare room, she holds the most intimate place in my heart. Lia had been so curious about chemistry, one of my favorite subjects. I like to imagine she's a successful scientist today. And I think of her every time I eat a bowl of macaroni and cheese.

Forty-Three Minutes
California, 2019

"Me time, here I come!" she thought with satisfaction. Dropping her daughter off at gymnastics, Marlene walked briskly down the block to her favorite coffee shop. Twice a week, the blogger mom frequented the same local coffee shop while ten-year-old Alicia attended gymnastics class. She ordered the same bone-dry flat white and occupied the same sunny corner seat on every visit. And placing her order at the coffee bar marked the beginning of her most precious personal time each week. No kids, no work. She had it all timed down to the minute: one minute to walk to the coffee shop and one minute to walk back to the studio. In between, forty-three blissful minutes of her favorite coffee and a good book.

Normally, Marlene's book was cracked open in one hand before she even sat down, coffee cup warming the other and eyes already trained on the page. But on the day Marlene broke from her routine and glanced around the café, she noticed a disheveled man sitting with two plastic bags propped lopsidedly at his feet. His dirty fingerless gloves wrapped around a paper cup of water as he glanced self-consciously in her direction. Marlene's mind's eye recognized him, and she realized he had probably been seated at the next table in previous weeks, though they had never exchanged a word. Seeing him eye her book, she asked with a hesitant smile, "Have you read this one?"

Tense eyes quickly glanced at the book cover, then back down at his chipped thumbnail as it picked nervously at the lip of his paper cup. "Uh, no. Not that one."

Marlene could sense a yearning in the man as he gazed back up at her with the quiet desperation of a person who has been alone for far too long. Though she longed to dive into her book, an urgent compassion seized her, and she asked kindly, "So what's your favorite book? I'll bet I've read it. I'm *addicted* to books!"

A smudged knee blinked in and out of sight, as his leg began to jiggle nervously. "I don't read much. Uh, I don't read at all. Actually, I can't really read. Never learned, not even as a kid."

—.—

As a child, Jeff was well liked and known as one of the more athletic boys in his elementary school class. "Yeah, you pick any sport, I killed it! The problem was...well, it was everything else," he said with a good-natured shrug.

For the once bright-eyed boy, a cycle of self-sabotage had started back in third grade. Slumped in the back corner of the classroom, the boy with the unruly Afro learned to adopt a sullen attitude, responding with sarcasm and disrespect when called upon. The teachers, not realizing Jeff's posture had been carefully constructed to cover his struggles with the curriculum, soon gave up trying to engage the boy and simply left him alone.

At home, Jeff's parents barely paid attention to him. He stayed outside after school, dribbling his basketball and scanning for pickup games around the neighborhood. Returning home after dark, he sometimes found leftovers in the fridge. Other times, he poured himself some cereal, crunching quietly as his parents got stoned in the den. "My folks? Those two just wake and bake all day. I coulda been run over by a truck, nobody know for days."

By the time he entered fourth grade, Jeff had fallen hopelessly behind. Most teachers ignored him entirely. One older woman seemed to take pleasure in criticizing him viciously, though she never sought to help him improve. He'll always remember her scathing comment, "I get paid whether you learn or not. Good thing, because I don't think you're teachable." Those words, dripping with disgust, struck deep and left an indelible scar. Upon hearing them, Jeff fell into a deep well of shame and came to believe the lie that he was, in fact, unteachable.

Eventually, although he was proud to have made the junior varsity basketball team freshman year, Jeff dropped out of school. "All I did was play ball. I didn't do no homework, never handed in a damned thing. My teachers *knew* I couldn't read, but nobody cared."

With a friend's help on the job application, Jeff got a job as a Dishwasher at a nearby restaurant. And because he was tall for his age, the near-fifteen-year-old passed for a recent high school graduate. Happily, as he started his new job, Jeff discovered that he liked his coworkers and the meal discount even more. The boy ate better than he had in years and learned quickly. He washed dishes and, in his downtime, swept floors and took out the trash.

As the now older Jeff spoke to Marlene in the coffee shop, she watched as he mentally transported back to a happier time. "I'd wash *mountains* of dishes and leave late...like, it was *way* after close. Then summa the boys would hang and kick it out back."

He remembered drinking beers with the crew after hours. Slouched on the curb or leaning against the dumpsters behind the restaurant, the guys joked with each other and passed the time in comfortable camaraderie. Contented, Jeff figured he'd stay at the restaurant, working his way up to Line Cook like some of the guys around him. He was already beginning to prep vegetables, and things were looking pretty good.

But then, everything changed when his parents were arrested. Taking a shaky sip of water, Jeff remembered bicycling home one night after close. His eyes widened when he realized the red and blue lights were flashing right in front of his apartment. Too afraid to stop, he cycled right by his house and stopped at the next complex. Half an hour later, the boy cautiously looped back toward his home, but again reversed course when he noticed the police car parked out front. Jeff was almost fifteen years old and fiercely independent. Yet, despite having taken care of himself for years, the boy knew he wouldn't be allowed to live alone. So, he never turned back. Over the next two years, he slept in the streets and worked his way up to line cook at work. "I wondered why nobody ever came looking for me," he commented reflectively. "But with all those kids already sleeping in the streets, I guess I was just one more."

— · —

As Jeff became accustomed to sleeping rough, he began to dream about having a place to live. Early one morning before garbage pickup, a small fabric bag caught his eye, resting on top of a trash can. The thin rope was broken, but the blue-green fabric was durable, and a sewn-in zipper seemed intact. He tied the pouch around his neck and began poking a few dollars in at the beginning of each week. "No matter what, I wasn't touching that money! It was my bank account—my future." By the time he was eighteen, the boy had figured out how to save about twenty-five dollars a week, and he watched with satisfaction as his little stockpile grew. When the bulge beneath Jeff's shirt became more pronounced, he was besieged with offers for every drug he could imagine, and some he'd never even heard of. "You got bank? Whatever you want, they got. But I saw what happened to folks who start doin' smack. I didn't need me none o' that. Trust me, though, sometimes I wanted it. I wanted it *bad.* But I knew once I started, there was no goin' back."

It was time to get off the streets. The energetic teen became increasingly paranoid as he fended off drug dealers, patting the lump under his shirt every few minutes for reassurance. Sometimes at work, Jeff locked himself in the restaurant's bathroom, the only place he could really ever be alone, and counted his money. One day, hunched over the toilet seat, he balanced a scrap of receipt paper on his knee, painstakingly adding numbers with his right hand as his left clutched the bills. Slowly, with concentration, the boy counted out a total of $275. Months of saving and eating nothing but discounted restaurant food had yielded more money than Jeff had ever seen at one time.

That same weekend, the young line cook bicycled around town, hunting for a cheap apartment. He couldn't read all the words, but he diligently scanned hand-painted signs propped in dusty windows. Then, when he caught sight of a painted cardboard sign that read "$275," Jeff jumped off his bike. The place was just a ten-minute ride from work. His heart soaring, the boy strode up to the door and knocked.

"But the sign says $275! I got that right here!" Jeff pleaded, fanning out the wrinkled dollars from his pouch. His elation had dissolved into frustration as the landlord explained about the security deposit. Seeing the boy's distress, the older man's heart softened, and he offered to take $500, instead of the full two months' rent, for the deposit.

"Another five hundred bucks! That's gonna take me another half year to save up!" the despondent teenager lamented, storming out and bicycling away furiously as he blinked back tears.

As Jeff resigned himself to the reality of another six months of street living, he began to sleep on his back at night, the reassuring weight of his pouch tucked firmly between his shoulder blades. On the night he was robbed, the little bag bulged with over four hundred dollars of hard-earned cash.

Awakening with a gasp, Jeff immediately knew something was gravely wrong. A metallic tang of fear filled his mouth as his body thrummed with adrenaline. "You move, he'll cut yo' sorry throat," wheezed a gravelly voice in his ear. Heavy knees shoved painfully into his armpits on either side, as a dark mass loomed from above. Jeff glimpsed the glint of a knife right before he felt it slice the cord around his neck. As hot blood gushed between his fingers, the boy pressed one hand against his wound while the other frantically grabbed for his assailant's shirt.

By morning, the wound had stopped bleeding. Jeff's shirt was stiff with rusty brown splatters, and an angry gash ran from just under his left jawbone to the inner edge of his collarbone. Filled with despair, he did the only thing he could. The despondent boy changed into his one clean shirt and headed to work.

The next few days passed in a gloomy blur, until Jeff unexpectedly caught sight of his familiar blue-green pouch, tied lopsidedly around a drifter's grimy neck. He didn't stop to think; all the pent-up anguish of losing a year's savings suddenly overflowed like boiling lava.

"All I remember is seein' him fall back and then punchin' his sick old face and then...nuthin," Jeff said, his eyes burdened with regret. He awoke in the Sacramento County jail and, unable to pay the $2,000 fine, soon found himself serving time at the local correctional center.

Then, a long six long months later, the young man found himself standing outside the prison with a small plastic bag and a $200 debit card. "They call that 'gate money' from the state, supposed to help with reentry, but where am I suppos'd to go? What am I suppos'd to do?" he said. Fighting a panic attack, Jeff bought a bus ticket and breathed shallowly the entire ride back to his old restaurant. The familiar building was the only place he had ever called home; the sounds and smells of it wrapped around him like a comfortable old blanket. But the faces staring back at him from the kitchen were unfamiliar. His manager had moved out of state, and the new one wanted nothing to do with a criminal. A few moments later, Jeff was back outside, blinking hard in the afternoon sun. "So, what now?" he thought.

Marlene glanced down at her watch and gasped as she realized gymnastics class was already over. She jumped up with a startled yelp, saying, "I'm so sorry! I have to go pick up my daughter! The time just flew by!"

Jeff's creased face broke into a grateful smile. "Sure am sorry I talked so much," he replied. "You didn't even read yo' book today. But...thanks."

Marlene hurriedly gathered her things and paused before she pushed open the glass door. "Jeff, I really enjoyed getting to know you. I'll see you again on Thursday?"

— • —

Mom and daughter reversed roles on the way home. Alicia, usually chatty and energized after class, sat in the back seat listening to her mom play back her conversation with the homeless man. Alicia sat, thoughtfully, pondering this new information that there were adults in the world who were unable to read. When they returned home, the fifth grader enthusiastically helped her mom scour the basement for old children's books.

That evening, the family dinner conversation revolved animatedly around Jeff. Marlene's husband, Matt, researched the U.S. literacy rate, sharing with the family that a government report showed that as of July 2019, one in five U.S. adults registered at the lowest literacy level. That meant forty-three million adults were classified as having low literacy or being functionally illiterate![1]

In fact, the family's home state, California, posted America's lowest literacy rate, with 23.1 percent of adults lacking basic prose literary skills.[2] Matt read from his iPhone, "Forty-three percent of adults with low literacy levels live in poverty, and seventy percent of adult welfare recipients register at those same literacy levels."[3] Digesting all they had learned, the family agreed that Marlene should try to help Jeff improve his reading skills. Alicia's little brother, just eight years old, proudly offered up his prized Dr. Seuss collection.

Three days later, as mother and daughter drove to gymnastics class, Alicia smiled proudly at her mom. She couldn't remember the last time she'd seen the polished blogger quite so nervous and giggled as her mom asked, "How did you learn how to read, honey? I can't remember how I taught you! What if I can't help Jeff?" Then, her voice raised in anxiety: "What if he has some undiagnosed learning disorder? I'm not *qualified* for this...what was I thinking?"

Yet, despite Marlene's concerns, despite the many ways in which life had beaten Jeff down, and despite that teacher's cruel voice from so long ago telling him he was "unteachable," the humble man approached his reading lessons with unwavering positivity. Slowly but surely, over the next few weeks, he graduated from *The Foot Book* to *Go, Dog. Go!*

Marlene, who had always felt her schedule was filled to the brim, found that she had something critical to offer after all. In fact, two forty-three-minute sessions twice a week turned out to be exactly what Jeff needed. Now, she eagerly anticipated her time with the older man, her quiet reading sessions long forgotten in the excitement of watching Jeff learn.

She respected how he never accepted charity, declining every time she offered to buy him food or drink. That's what made it all the more special when he shyly accepted a celebration Frappuccino on the day he successfully read a line from her son's favorite book, "There's a nureau in my bureau." They laughed together when he sheepishly asked, "So, what the hell's a nureau, anyway?"

As summer approached and school began to wind down, Alicia prepared to swap her twice-weekly gymnastics class for summer sleepaway camp. Around the same time, Marlene helped Jeff fill out a series of job applications. And two weeks after that, the blogger enjoyed the best flat white she'd ever tasted. As she turned her coffee cup to read her name, handwritten in his familiar slant, Jeff beamed at her with pride from behind the espresso machine.

A Friend
Arkansas, 2016

"Always knew she was a slut."

"What a whore. Totally FU."

"Maybe I'll get her part...preggers can't play Rebecca Gibbs."

"NW she's already @ 4 mo!"

Josie shook her head in disbelief as she swiftly thumbed through dozens of message bubbles. The honey-blond teen had just finished swiping on a second coat of mascara when she picked up the vibrating phone that had slowly inched across the bathroom counter with every incoming message. She couldn't decide which was more shocking: that her friend Haylee had gotten pregnant or that everyone was reacting so horribly. Thumbs poised over the phone, Josie thought about what she wanted to say, but a quick glance at the upper-right corner of her screen told her she was already running late to work. Sliding the phone in her back pocket, she took one last peek in the mirror, grabbed her purse, and ran out the door.

As the ponytailed girl drove to the Walmart Supercenter for her Saturday shift, she could feel the phone buzzing insistently in her back pocket. "Poor Haylee," she thought, as her red Prius turned into the expansive parking lot. If social media was already exploding like this today, Monday was going to be an absolute nightmare.

A junior in high school, Josie juggled a hectic schedule of cheerleading practice, drama, and work on the weekends. The back seat of her car told her entire life's story. A half-zipped backpack had spilled its contents all over the floor. Empty Chick-fil-A wrappers peeked from under her cheer uniform, and a gift for her boyfriend, Brandon, sat wrapped on the seat for tonight.

It was going to be a totally awesome weekend. Josie was planning to rush home after her shift to quickly shower and change. Her boyfriend had booked a reservation at Bordinos on trendy Dickson Street, to celebrate their one-year anniversary. The little black dress she had bought for the occasion was already laid out on her bed, and the timing was just perfect! His parents were at their lake house this weekend, so the whole house was theirs. Josie's heart beat a little faster, and a luminous smile stretched across her face as she walked across the store.

In the back room, Josie quickly placed her things in her locker and slipped the blue vest on, just as her frazzled manager popped his head in. "Hey, Jos, I need you in the maternity section today. There are already three racks by the fitting rooms waiting to be recovered."

That next hour, as Josie methodically relocated articles of clothing from the rolling racks back to their rightful places in the store, she silently mouthed her lines, mentally rehearsing for the school play. Then, thinking back to the day when casting decisions had been made, Josie remembered how thrilled she had been to hear her name called for the lead role in *Our Town*. She remembered squeezing Haylee, who would play her sister. The girls were also in the same chemistry class and had paired up as lab partners. Haylee, with her curly brown hair and gorgeous dimples, had turned out to be a really sweet girl. Discovering that both their boyfriends were on the football team, they had even talked about double-dating for junior prom in a couple of months.

But how *was* Haylee? Would she really have to give up her spot in the play? When would the baby start to show? Was she going to be throwing up all the time? Josie gazed at a pair of dark-washed maternity jeggings in her hands, thinking, "I can't even imagine what that's going to be like." With a sigh and a quick shake of her head, the teenager shifted her thoughts back to the lines she still had to memorize.

A few hours later, vest tucked back in her locker and purse slung over her shoulder, Josie yelled a cheerful "Goodnight, everyone!" as she left the back room, preparing to head home. But as she passed the maternity section on her right, the girl's feet suddenly slowed. A new thought struck her so forcefully, it left her physically winded. What if she and Brandon had gotten pregnant? There was that one time the condom broke.... What if *she* had become the subject of those horrible texts?

Unexpectedly overwhelmed with a combination of cold fear and warm compassion, Josie quickly rummaged through the racks until she found that cute pair of jeggings. Before she could overthink it, the girl walked briskly to the checkout, pulled out her associate discount card, and paid for the jeggings.

That evening in the warm glow of the restaurant, Josie and Brandon held hands across the table. Everything was just perfect. Her new LBD fit like a glove, her boyfriend looked (and smelled!) amazing, and they had just traded thoughtful anniversary gifts. He said with a wink, "Ready to go? Dessert's at my place." Haylee's drama was soon forgotten as the young couple strolled out the door, the boy's warm hand pressing gently on the small of her back.

— · —

But on Monday morning as Josie parked in the school lot, the plastic bag sitting beside her reminded the girl of her impulsive weekend purchase. "How am I going to give these to her? That's totally weird. I should just return them. OMG what was I thinking?"

Shaking her head with a sigh, undecided, Josie shoved the bag deep in her backpack, slammed the car door shut, and pushed through the school doors just as the first bell rang.

Once again, the popular teen forgot about the jeggings as she caught up with friends and gushed about her amazingly romantic weekend. But as the girls ran into the locker room to change for gym class, Josie caught sight of a red-eyed Haylee. Leaning across the narrow bench between them, Josie asked, "Hey, are you OK?"

Haylee glanced at her defaced locker, shook her head miserably, seemingly too choked up to utter a reply, and turned to leave the locker room. Josie's eyes drifted from her friend's receding frame back to the locker across from her. The word "slut" had been viciously scratched into the ugly tan steel.

Josie stood helplessly, not knowing if she should run after her friend or just let her be. Suddenly, she remembered the jeggings. Reaching into her backpack, she pulled out the bag and hurriedly shoved it into Haylee's locker. Feeling just the tiniest bit better, she closed her own locker door and ran out to class.

By the end of that first excruciating week, Haylee had pulled out of the school play. Brutal rumors swirled about who the father was, and slut-shaming had begun in earnest. Josie sat silently, staring fixedly at her phone as her lunch table gossiped about Haylee. She was appalled at her own friend group. These were girls she'd grown up with; they had shared sleepovers, laughed and cried together...and now they huddled and furtively giggled as they texted "Just kill yourself" to

Haylee's phone. How could they possibly think this was funny? Sinking even farther down into her seat, Josie miserably waited for lunchtime to be over.

By the second week, Haylee had taken down her Instagram account, but not before her wall on the platform was filled with withering posts like "Don't stop at the baby, abort yourself" and "You deserve to die." Josie started checking Instagram less and less, repulsed by the nastiness that spread like a virus on her social media channels.

— • —

One Friday afternoon after cheer practice, Josie grabbed her water bottle and began walking off the field with her friends. Glancing at the cheerful faces around her, she took a deep breath and asked, "So why are you guys terrorizing Haylee anyway? She's never done anything to you!" Time suddenly seemed to slow as her friends turned to face her, one by one. Crinkled, smiling eyes suddenly narrowed, zeroing in on her to express outrage and disbelief. Drawing closer to one another, the girls menacingly circled Josie as one member of the squad angrily spat, "What, you want to take *her* side? You want to join the 3H club?"

"What's the 3H club?" Josie asked, perplexed.

"Aren't you on IG? *Everyone* knows about the 3H club! Hang Haylee the ho!" The cheerleaders, looking so incongruously perky on the sunny green field as they gathered around Josie, tittered gleefully as they pulled out their phones. And that was how Josie learned about the online competition to see who could force Haylee to kill herself.

Josie's face felt frozen as her blood ran cold, her lips stretched tightly somewhere between a smile and a grimace. The other girls drifted away, scrolling through their social media feeds, shrieking with laughter at some of the latest comments.

The cheerleader stood rooted on the field, her mind whirling. With apprehension, she pulled out her phone and logged back into Instagram for the first time in days. Then, Josie's eyes widened as she read one malicious comment after another. The school seemed to have turned into an angry online mob. Boys were claiming to have slept with Haylee, and girls were posting poisonous barbs like "She deserves to get raped." Josie felt her stomach flip and turn, as her thumb scrolled on and on. She felt trapped like a hamster on a horrible wheel, desperately wanting to look away but unable to tear her eyes away from the screen. Was this how Haylee felt all the time?

Josie had noticed the pregnant girl looking increasingly despondent at school. Though Haylee's belly had started to round out, her face had become gaunt, her cheeks hollow, and the circles under her eyes so dark, they looked like bruises. The slut-shaming and endless taunting had to be taking its toll.

The next day at work, Josie used her associate discount to buy a cute maternity top, planning to sneak it into Haylee's locker before gym class on Monday. She hoped these secret gifts might lift her friend's spirits and also lessen the crushing weight pressing uncomfortably on her own chest.

But after everyone had run out into the gym, Haylee seemed to linger in the locker room. Knowing class was about to start, Josie deliberately turned her back, pretending to look for something in her backpack as she waited for the now showing teen to leave the room. But when she quickly peeked over her shoulder, the pregnant teen was seated quietly on the bench, staring inquisitively at her.

"You're the one leaving me clothes in my locker, right?"

Josie turned cautiously toward the girl. She adopted an overly casual tone: "Um, yeah. It's no big deal. I work at Walmart and use my associate discount. Like, I'm working in the store anyways."

Then, more hesitantly, she asked, "Am I picking the right sizes? Are they fitting OK?"

Haylee laughed self-consciously, gesturing at her jeggings. "They're just starting to get tight, but I've definitely gotten good use out of these."

After a long, awkward pause, the pregnant teenager finally asked, "Why, Josie? Why are you buying me stuff?"

The thundering echo of forty sneakers pounded across the gymnasium and filled the embarrassed silence. Class had started, but no one had come looking for the girls yet. Josie suddenly blurted out, "I *hate* what they're doing! I can't believe everyone's acting this way, and I hate the 3H club. Everyone's being so horrible; I just don't know what to do!"

Haylee's hazel eyes welled up with tears. In a quavering voice, she said, "Thank you for the clothes. But honestly, Josie, I couldn't care less what I wear right now. What I *need* is a friend." As the tears spilled onto her pale cheeks, she looked beseechingly up at the cheerleader from her seat. "Will you just be my friend?"

Josie's heart constricted painfully as Haylee dropped her curly-haired head into her hands and sobbed. From as early as she could remember, Josie had been known as a "good friend." She was a great listener and always remembered her friends' birthdays. Now, she blinked back tears as the harsh realization washed over her with chilling clarity: she had been a *terrible* friend. She had watched Haylee get tormented in school and cyberbullied. Suddenly, she recalled the words of Martin Luther King Jr. from social studies class earlier that week: "In the end, we will remember not the words of our enemies, but the silence of our friends." Wordlessly, Josie dropped to her knees in front of her friend.

She reached out and grasped Haylee's hands. "Yes," Josie said quietly, looking up into her friend's tearful face. As Haylee's red-rimmed eyes connected with hers, Josie continued, the words rushing out in a cathartic flood: "I'm sorry. I'm so sorry. I've been an *awful* friend. I was afraid of becoming a target, so I didn't say anything. And that probably made you feel even *more* alone. And then, when I saw what everyone was writing online, I just couldn't deal!"

Haylee burst out laughing through her tears. "*You* couldn't deal? Imagine being *me*! It's like I have this insane addiction to seeing what everyone's saying...*all the time*. It's completely *sick*! Boys I've never even met are saying they slept with me!"

"Well, it's time to tell them a new story," Josie said with conviction, as she stood up and shook out her legs. "And let's get to gym before we end up with detention." Both girls wiped the tears from their faces and straightened their shoulders, turning toward the door.

The entire class paused mid-calisthenics when the girls walked in, hand in hand. And the next day, when Josie plopped down beside Haylee in the cafeteria, the murmuring swelled to an angry buzz. And just as it had on that Saturday when she'd first heard the news about Haylee, Josie's vibrating phone inched across the table, alive with incoming messages. She finally picked it up when Brandon's name caught her eye. Haylee glanced at her anxiously, suggesting, "Maybe this isn't a good idea. Just answer Brandon's call and go sit with your friends."

Josie glared at Haylee and declared resolutely, "You *are* my friend. If Brandon doesn't want to sit with me, it's his loss." She quickly texted back, "B, come sit with us xo." But as she scanned the room, her boyfriend only briefly caught her eye before guiltily turning away.

Over lunch that day, sitting in what felt like an invisible bubble at their own table, Josie learned more about Haylee's situation. "Oh my God!" she exclaimed, slapping her hands on the table. The baby is *his*?! Why didn't you just tell everyone, and why isn't he saying anything?"

With a grim shake of her head, Haylee insisted, "Do *not* tell anyone. If he doesn't want anyone to know and won't take responsibility, I don't *want* him in the baby's life." Again, Josie couldn't help but wonder what Brandon would have done if they'd ended up in the same situation. Seeing him sitting with Haylee's ex at the football table, she shook her head in disgust. She turned back toward her friend. "OK, tell me something good," she said. "Do you know if it's a boy or a girl?"

At this, Haylee's face dimpled, and she yanked her bag up from where she'd deposited it by her feet. Sifting through a pile of papers, she proudly handed a gray photo across the table to Josie. "It's a girl!"

Eyes wide, Josie gushed, "This is the cutest thing I've ever seen! Look, I can see her little fingers and her nose! She looks just *like* you!" Impulsively, she asked if she could snap a photo of the ultrasound image. Just then, the bell rang, and the friends parted ways as they headed to their respective classes. Haylee looked more upbeat than she had in weeks, and she didn't even pull her phone out to see what people were saying.

On the other side of the school as she made her way to class, Josie scrolled through her messages.

"WTF girl, why ru sitting with the slut?"

"Dude, not cool. Get ur ass over here."

And on and on it went. With a deep sigh, she scanned the names. It seemed her friends from cheer and drama were going to be the most vocal. "Well," she thought, "bring it on." Once the tenacious girl made a decision, she stuck with it. It's how she had made the cheer squad and landed the lead role in the school play. And in this case, she knew without a doubt that she was doing the right thing. What she had to offer was exactly what Haylee needed. She was going to be the friend that the teenager needed, and let the haters hate.

As everyone congregated for drama after school, a barrage of questions assaulted the lead actress. Thinking ahead, Josie had already expected the onslaught and had decided not to defend her friend. Instead, she held up her cell phone. "Check this out! I've never seen an ultrasound before. How cute is *this*?! Her baby's going to be a *girl!*" she shared enthusiastically. Immediately, curiosity overtook the group as Josie's phone was passed around.

As she drove home from drama that evening, Josie called Haylee. "Hey, I have an idea! Are you OK if I share the baby's ultrasound online? You should have *seen* everyone at drama! I flashed the photo and all that hate disappeared in a *heartbeat!* Everyone thought she was so *cute!*" With the intuition of a seasoned marketer, Josie launched what she secretly called her "friend campaign" that same evening.

Pretty soon, kids were stopping by their lunch table to ask questions about the baby. The same girls who had posted "Die slut" now wanted to feel the baby kick, gasping in wonder when they felt a little foot push against their hands. With Haylee's permission, Josie posted an online poll to help determine the baby girl's name. And miraculously, not a single person posted a mean comment. The school had left behind its ugliness, all because one teenage girl had had the courage to be a real friend.

And a few months later, when Haylee gave birth to a healthy baby girl, Josie was the first to receive a text. Superimposed on the photo of a scrunched-up, red-faced baby, a thought bubble asked, "Will you be my godmother?"

—REFLECTION—

Though I possessed few resources as a college junior, the extra couch in my New York studio apartment was all that Lia needed. Years later in California, Jeff secured his first steady job in years because Marlene invested forty-three minutes, twice a week, to help him learn to read. And in Arkansas, a teenage girl gathered the courage to offer exactly what another student needed: friendship.

So, whether it's a spare room, time, or energy, everyone has something to offer. And whether it can be extended effortlessly or it requires great bravery and sacrifice, each of us has the opportunity to put forth exactly what someone else needs.

As you finish reading this chapter, look around your surroundings with fresh eyes. Because in fact, giving starts exactly where we are.

Who might need something you are equipped to provide? What resources do you have available, whether it's an extra set of gardening gloves or old children's books in the basement? What pockets of time do you have available, though it may feel as though you're already overly committed? Look again and consider the resources at your disposal. Sometimes we are able to make dramatic changes in our lives to meet a need, and other times, we can be just as effective with what feels like small investments.

—·—

The following questions and exercises will help you break down your Offer, by identifying what resources, skills, and capabilities you are uniquely positioned to put forward.

1. Let's start with identifying your current and desired end state on a simple value scale.

HOW MUCH DO YOU CONTRIBUTE VERSUS CONSUME ON A DAILY BASIS?

1—I am a total consumer and don't actively contribute in any meaningful way.

2—I consume more than I contribute.

3—I consume about as much as I contribute.

4—I contribute more than I consume.

5—I am single-mindedly focused on my contribution and minimize my consumption in every way that I can.

Consume			Contribute	
1	2	3	4	5

IN THE FUTURE, WHAT WOULD YOU LIKE THIS SCALE TO LOOK LIKE?

Consume			Contribute	
1	2	3	4	5

Figure 1.1

If you're interested in shifting your value equation to the right on this scale and stepping up your contribution, you can start with a self-assessment. Identifying and naming what you have to offer begin with getting to know yourself. And as you assess yourself in the four areas below, you will begin to narrow in on your unique Offer, and later use it to define your social legacy.

Figure 1.2

2. What are your capabilities? These are your strengths, your areas of expertise. As you list your capabilities, here are some questions to help you get started.

- When and where do you excel?
- When people come to you for help, what do they seek?
- What do you do better than most people around you?
- What skills do you possess, about which you sometimes think, "I should do something more with these"?

Some examples of capabilities are:

- **Business acumen**—you intuitively grasp different areas of business operations and how they are interconnected, to make sound, strategic business decisions.
- **Communication and presentation skills**—whether through oral or written communication, you are able to express complex ideas clearly and compellingly.
- **Conflict management**—you recognize and deal with disputes in a rational and effective manner, managing negativity and extracting positive outcomes from strife.
- **Direction and delegation**—you innately identify the right resources for the right tasks, assigning work scope and articulating responsibility with precision.
- **Envisioning**—you are able to imagine something that doesn't yet exist but should, galvanizing others around that vision and grounding it in stretching targets.
- **Languages and culture**—you understand and speak multiple languages. Further, you are able to recognize and bridge individual and cultural differences to foster empathy and understanding.
- **Medical or emergency training**—you feel confident dealing with injuries and respond with level-headedness in emergency situations.
- **Negotiation**—you self-monitor and process quickly under pressure, and are adept at finding the win-win solution that leaves multiple parties satisfied with an outcome.
- **Organizational management**—you assess and leverage assets and resources effectively, implementing structures and processes that accelerate workflow and improve employee satisfaction.
- **People management**—you identify the right people for the right roles and establish the right motivation and support to enable business performance and job satisfaction.

- **Political savvy**—you are self- and socially aware, understanding the environment around you and what motivates people. You sincerely enjoy having interpersonal influence and networking.
- **Problem-solving**—you deftly analyze complex challenges, distilling critical information to pinpoint a useful holistic solution.
- **Project management**—you are supremely organized and enjoy planning, mapping, and managing the resources necessary to deliver an end result within a finite timescale and budget.
- **Technological literacy**—you are fluent with digital devices and information, and are able to design and use technology to access, create, manage, and integrate content.
- Other _____

YOUR MOST MEANINGFUL CAPABILITIES ARE (CHOOSE UP TO 3):

_____

_____

_____

3. What are your passion areas? These are the activities that feed your soul and give you joy. Here's a tip: check your calendar, because these are the activities that you will always make time for. Here are some questions to help you get started.

- What makes you laugh, cry, and sing?
- What keeps you awake at night, and what do you dream about during the day?
- What would you be willing to go to jail for, or even die for?

Here are some examples of passion areas.

- Art
- Blogging and writing
- Books
- Cooking
- Dance
- Exercise, fitness, and nutrition
- Gaming
- Gardening
- Hospitality
- Movies
- Music
- Outdoor activities: camping, hiking, fishing
- Photography
- Pop culture
- Running
- Yoga
- Other _____

YOUR GREATEST PASSIONS ARE (CHOOSE UP TO 3):

_____

_____

_____

4. What makes you unique? These are the characteristics that set you apart and make you uniquely you. They can relate to your background, personality, or appearance, and might be rooted in your family, education, vocation, or even painful experiences from your past. Here are some questions to help you get started.

- What do those who know you well tell you that they love about you?
- How might they describe the driving force in your life, or your pet cause?
- What experiences have you had that many others have not yet lived through?
- What have you seen and accomplished in your life?
- What have you been recognized for?

> **What if you were grateful for your pain?**
> *What has it taught you?*
> *How has it refined you to be who you are today?*
> *What if you were meant to go through that experience?*
> *What if that is the thing that makes you unique?*

- What kinds of ads does your social media serve up? Those are built on an algorithm that accounts for all your online activity, so they may provide uniquely unbiased insight!

Some examples of your unique characteristics might be:

- **Agile**—you are able to move and think quickly, and love doing so.
- **Attentive**—people seek you out because they feel heard and seen when they're with you.
- **Colorful**—you add fun and texture to everyday situations.
- **Courageous**—you exhibit bravery and speak when others remain silent.

- **Curious**—you possess an unquenchable thirst to understand how and why things work the way they do.
- **Empathetic**—you sense and understand the feelings of others to the point where you are able to see and experience the world from their point of view.
- **Helpful**—you are the first to notice and assist someone in need.
- **Humorous**—you have the ability to lighten the mood and make people laugh.
- **Independent**—you think critically and form your own opinions. Not easily swayed by others, you assume responsibility for your thoughts and decisions.
- **International**—you have seen a broad cross section of the globe, which has informed your worldview.
- **Media maven**—you have a knack for creating and sharing content that others find useful and engaging.
- **Motivational**—you possess the ability to rouse and galvanize people, inspiring them to take action.
- **Patient**—you remain composed under all circumstances and are known for your tolerance and deliberation.
- **Persistent**—regardless of the obstacle or challenge, your grit, resilience, and strength of character motivate you to persevere.
- **Survivor**—you have successfully coped with and have come out the other side of unusually challenging circumstances.
- Other _____

THE CHARACTERISTICS AND EXPERIENCES THAT MOST MAKE YOU UNIQUE ARE (CHOOSE UP TO 3):

_____

_____

_____

5. What resources do you possess? These are assets and materials that are readily available to you. It's worth noting that unlike skills, passions, and unique characteristics, resources are not always renewable. They can be gathered, used, and depleted over time. To help catalogue resources you might have available, I have created three categories: time, energy, and wealth and physical assets.

Time. Arguably our most precious resource, it's democratically available to everyone in the same limited quantity. We each get the same twenty-four hours a day, though some of us may feel we never have enough time for the things we would like to do. We may gripe, "There's no time to exercise" or, "I don't have enough time for lunch." But since time is a constant, our issue is not that we don't have enough of it, but rather that we aren't prioritizing the things that we should.

Take a look at your schedule; in fact, you'll find that you are always able to make time for the things you really value. So, ask yourself: are you truly maximizing every hour of every day? Might you be allocating your time more frivolously than you do your physical resources? More important, should you? Because while physical resources can be replenished, once time has passed, it's gone forever. Marlene had always felt she didn't have enough time to do what she called "social work," yet just two forty-three-minute sessions twice a week completely changed her and Jeff's lives.

So, how are you spending your time? Count up and divide a twenty-four-hour block into sleep, work, and other life priorities. Using the circle below, create a pie chart that visualizes where your time gets invested. What does your day look like? What available capacity might be carved out in your schedule? When, specifically, is this free time available?

How I invest my twenty-four-hour day:

Figure 1.3

As a reference, here is an example of how I invest my own time on an average weekday.

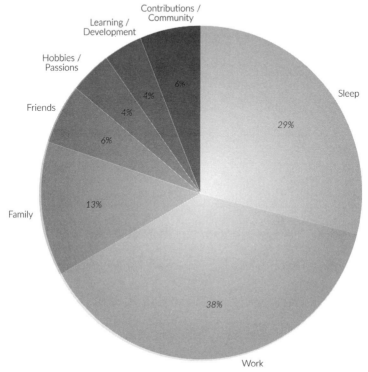

Figure 1.4

Now, consider how you might adjust your investment of time. Perhaps you find your allocation of time to be just right. If so, that's great! If not, use the circle below to create a pie chart that illustrates your ideal state. What would you adjust? With this exercise, we're endowing time with a physical quality. I find that when I treat time like something tangible—say, like cold, hard cash in my wallet—I regard it as a more valuable resource, to be spent with a higher degree of intentionality.

How I would like to invest my day:

Figure 1.5

Great job! Now, before we move on, please take a moment to reflect on what you have learned about yourself, and how you might modify the way you allocate your time. Last but not least, consider whether time is fundamental to your Offer.

WHAT I LEARNED ABOUT HOW I INVEST MY TIME:

_____

_____

HOW I PLAN TO ADJUST HOW MY TIME IS SPENT:

_____

_____

Energy. Defined as the effort, enthusiasm, creativity, and consideration we put into a task, energy may be the cornerstone of your Offer. How do you react when you witness an injustice or experience a negative emotion? Do you get fired up and find that nothing quells your discomfort like taking action against the affront? When Josie found herself in this position, she gathered her courage and her spirit to stand up for her friend. Like her, are you interested in pouring your energy into things that are good, noble, excellent, and worthy?

How might you become more mindful of how you invest your energy? Like time, energy is an important, finite resource that we may not treat with the consideration it deserves because of its intangibility. So, let's try to make it more tangible.

Using the chart on the following page, take a moment and reflect on where you put your energy. How much vitality do you expend on things you can control, compared to things that are out of your control? And how much of your spirit do you pour into the negative, compared to the positive?

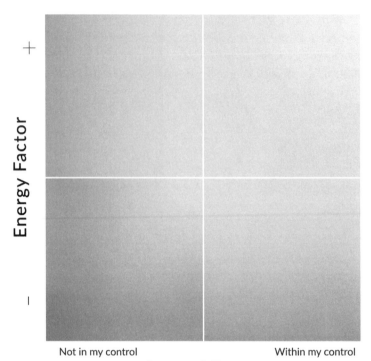

Control Factor

Figure 1.6

Excellent! Now, go back to the chart and circle the focus areas that you would like to adjust. Are you investing precious energy in negative things that are outside of your control? What if you were able to let those elements go and reallocate that energy elsewhere? Do you find your upper-right box sparser than you might like? Perhaps that's a signal that positive energy might be a key pillar of your Offer.

Before we move on to the next resource, please take a moment to reflect on what you have learned about yourself, and how you might reshape the way you invest your energy. Last but not least, consider whether energy is fundamental to your Offer.

WHAT I LEARNED ABOUT HOW I INVEST MY ENERGY:

_____

_____

HOW I PLAN TO ADJUST WHERE AND HOW MY ENERGY IS SPENT:

_____

_____

Wealth and physical assets. While money is the first thing that might come to mind, we each possess a plethora of physical resources that may be the exact thing someone else needs. Yet, identifying those assets may appear to be a daunting task, so check out the framework below that is designed to help you methodically inventory your possessions.

> *What if you had just one week left to live?*
>
> *What are you hanging on to that you really don't need?*
>
> *What if that exact thing would make someone else's final week more comfortable or life-giving?*

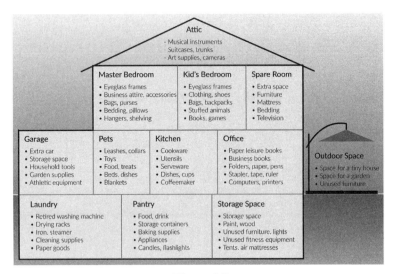

Figure 1.7

Where did you catalogue the most unused or forgotten resources in your possession? Where did you observe excess that someone else might put to good use? Please take a moment to list the resources you might be willing to offer up. Not only can you benefit someone who needs just that thing, but you will also discover the joy of decluttering and tidying, and of simplifying your own life.

THE PHYSICAL POSSESSIONS I DON'T NEED OR USE:

_____

_____

A Perfect Fit

Wonderful! Now let's put it all together. Your Offer will integrate your particular capabilities and passions with what makes you uniquely you and the resources you have available.

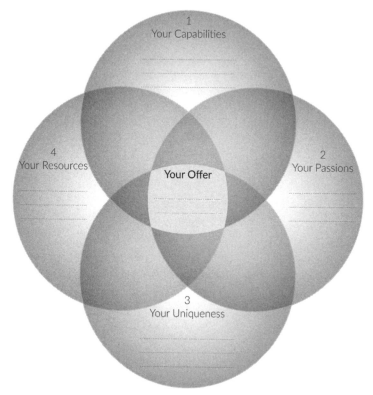

Figure 1.8

As you review the particular combination that defines your Offer, does anything begin to crystallize in the center of your chart? You might not identify something that perfectly integrates all four bubbles, but perhaps a combination of two or three words will evoke an idea. As your Offer begins to take shape, don't worry if it isn't particularly concrete or precise. We will continue to work on it through the chapters that follow.

What are your non-negotiables?
They may be physical, financial, emotional, or spiritual. For instance, mine are sleep and exercise, my husband's is time in nature, and my daughter's is quality reading time. What about you?

- *What do you need to protect your physical wellness? Consider how much sleep you need and what fuels your energy.*
- *What insulates your emotional wellness? Consider what stirs your heart and reduces stress for you.*
- *What maintains your spiritual balance? Consider those things that help you remain centered.*
- *What about financial comfort? What is necessary to get you out of survival mode?*

Now, what's left? Might what remains contribute to or become your Offer?

—RESOURCES—

Are you interested in helping homeless teens like Lia? Call the National Runaway Safeline at 1-800-RUNAWAY to locate a teen runaway shelter near you. Or you can volunteer on a crisis line, connecting with runaway, homeless, and at-risk youths in their most vulnerable moments. Thanks to crisis line volunteers and donations, the National Runaway Safeline is available twenty-four hours a day, 365 days a year. Sign up at https://www.eventbrite .com/e/nrs-volunteer-orientation-become-a-crisis-line-volunteer -tickets-29862247787?aff=Website.

Like Marlene, would you be interested in helping struggling adults through tutoring or teaching? Sign up to be a basic-skills tutor or teach adult basic education at a homelessness facility near you. Don't feel comfortable doing one-on-one tutoring? Consider donating old books and extra office supplies to a shelter.

Did Haylee's situation trigger you? Here are some ways you can help fight cyberbullying. Visit cybersmile.org to learn more about and help combat cyberbullying. Teens and young adults ages thirteen to twenty-four can access resources and help at stompoutbullying.org.

If someone you know is feeling hopeless or depressed, have him or her call the National Suicide Prevention Lifeline at 1-800-273-TALK (8255).

CHAPTER 2

The Burn of Indignation

An unrelenting sense of outrage defines the shape of your Offense.

*"The only thing necessary for the triumph of evil
is for good men to do nothing."*

—EDMUND BURKE

Bruises
Ohio, 2001

"But tomorrow, I'm going to be homeless!" The anguished words sailed across the salon as the room grew suddenly quiet. The bright-eyed girl who had greeted me at the front counter now sat crumpled in despair as tears poured down her face.

Sprinkled across the large, open room, five of us perched on black salon chairs of varying heights. The older woman seated on my left quickly closed the softcover book she'd been holding, her skin pulled taut at the temples and hair neatly secured in evenly distributed pink rollers. I strained to see who the girl was speaking with, as my colorist crisply folded another section of wet, color-drenched hair into a piece of foil. Setting aside my BlackBerry device, I watched as the salon owner sadly shook her head and responded to the girl: "I'm sorry, I just can't give you an advance. I took you on for a trial period, and you only started two weeks ago."

Now, with all eyes riveted to the front desk, it felt as though a spotlight had been turned on, transforming the counter into center stage. Looking around at the concerned faces, the girl, Devon, began to share her emotional story to the room full of strangers. She'd just moved to Cincinnati with her boyfriend of five years, Michael, because his cousin had gotten him a great job as an auto mechanic on the west side. Yes, he'd had to drop out of school, but everyone knew there were hardly any jobs back home in their backward little county. Sure, she'd dropped out of school, too, but it didn't matter, because just as soon as they could, Devon and Michael were going to get married and start making babies. But until then, she sure couldn't live at Michael's cousin's place. Devon was saving herself for marriage, and her parents would *kill* her if they found out the kids were sleeping in the same place! But who knew that apartments, even teeny-tiny closets like the ones she'd found in the papers, cost so much in the big city! She'd blown nearly five hundred dollars at a motel in just two weeks, savings that she had expected to last for a month.

The assortment of women, sitting with their hair in turbans, plastic wrap, or foil, had been strangers upon entering just an hour prior. But now as we faced this heartbroken girl, the group rallied into the kind of instant community one can uniquely find in midwestern beauty salons.

"Girl, get yourself home tonight! You're still a baby. You let your parents take care of you."

"Uh-huh! Go back to school and get your diploma first. He'll wait for you if he's a good man."

"You won't go home? Well, tell him to get you a nice apartment—that's the least he can do, with you up and leaving everything to follow him."

Eventually, one black cutting cape was whisked off after another, as we emerged with bouncy curls, fresh color, and shiny bobs. Handing my credit card to Devon, I quietly asked, "So, seriously. What are you going to do?"

Half an hour later as Devon packed her bags and returned the motel key to the office, I stood under a flickering hallway light and emailed my husband that I was going to be late for dinner. Oh, and could he make up the bed in our spare room?

Devon couldn't believe we actually lived in a town called Loveland. "That's the most romantic thing I ever heard!" she exclaimed.

She stared in awe as the garage door rolled up. "You can park both cars inside!" she marveled.

Her wide eyes took in the flowered wallpaper and dark green border we hadn't yet stripped in the kitchen. "Look how pretty! This kitchen's as big as my mama's whole family room!"

But when she entered the spare room, she suddenly began to shake her head. "I don't know. I don't think I can stay here. It doesn't feel right. Y'all don't even know me."

Then, in a tiny voice, almost as an afterthought: "You're not gonna *murder* me in my sleep, are you?"

— · —

As newlyweds, my husband and I were excited to share our first home with Devon. Also, she provided the perfect excuse for me to finally decorate that extra room. The house was furnished mostly with mismatched college pieces from our previous apartments. But as I had recently accepted a job at the Procter & Gamble company in the prestigious fabric care division, grown-up furniture felt like an official, affirmative step into adulthood.

That Saturday, Devon was out all day with Michael. It was the perfect opportunity to decorate her room. Minki and I made it a "date day," driving to Pier 1, Cost Plus World Market, and Walmart, buying everything we thought our guest would need to feel at home. I'll always remember my husband commenting as we waited in line at the store, "It's not enough for her to feel comfortable; she should feel *valued*. For these few months, we have the chance to build into her self-worth." That was one of many moments over these past twenty years when I felt the world pause for a brief moment as I gazed at my partner with a newly deepened respect, and a profound love.

That evening, I made Devon tie on a cloth blindfold before we walked her to her room. When she excitedly whipped off the scrap of fabric from her eyes, the teenager screamed in delight, taking in the vibrant bedspread, Asian-inspired wardrobe, and funky red chandelier hanging overhead. Throwing her arms around me, she whispered in my ear, "Thank you! I feel like the luckiest girl ever!" Her joy was contagious, and as she gazed at the room in the muted glow of the ruby light, I leaned into my husband, grinning with satisfaction.

The next morning, as we enjoyed a lazy breakfast together, I asked Devon if she wanted to have Michael over sometime. We were curious to meet him, and secretly I wondered if he was really as wonderful as she claimed he was. When she heard the suggestion, her normally expressive eyes dropped to her plate, pale eyelashes fluttering as she slowly chewed her food. "Um, he's really busy at the shop. And when he has downtime, he just likes to veg out and play video games."

Recognizing Devon's discomfort, my husband responded lightheartedly, "Well, I guess this wouldn't be the place for him, then. We don't even have a TV!"

Those four months with Devon flew by like a joyful snap. The girl was fun and bubbly, and the three of us often cooked up crazy creations for dinner together. In the evenings, we'd play a version of Pictionary with rules we'd made up for three players, or she and Minki would work on a puzzle at the dining table while I caught up on emails. Michael stopped by a few times to pick up his girlfriend, but he was always in a hurry and sometimes didn't even come up to the door. I remember Devon's casual response when I once admonished, "He really should pick you up at the door. Women don't come running when men honk at us."

She squeezed me in a tight hug and laughed, saying, "Oh, Emily. You're so old-fashioned! I don't mind at all," but then gasped and scurried out the door as an insistent *beep-beep* sounded from the driveway.

One Friday, I returned home, surprised to find Devon already cooking dinner. Something was definitely up. She'd lit candles and even prepared a floppy little centerpiece with flowers from the backyard. As we sat down to eat, Devon seemed unusually formal. She thanked us for welcoming her into our home and then, her eyes glowing, the words she'd been holding back all day came tumbling out with a gush: "Michael asked me to marry him! I'm gonna be his wife!"

The young couple had realized that if they put their money together, they could finally afford an apartment. Michael was sick of sleeping on his cousin's sofa and hated driving all the way up to Loveland to pick up Devon.

"Devon, I'm happy if you're happy. But hon, can you even *get* married this young?" I asked. That evening, I did some internet research, learning that our houseguest would be legally categorized as a child bride. I became curious about American laws around marriage. What was the definition of a child bride? As an American, I admit that the phrase brought to mind young, helpless girls in Third World countries, but Minki and I soon learned that child brides were legal in most of the United States, too.

The Burn of Indignation

We discovered that laws vary in different states. In fact, many years later and only in 2018, Delaware would become the first state to ban child marriage without exceptions, followed by New Jersey in the same year.[1] So, back in 2002, while at least half of our states reported a minimum marriage age, I was shocked to learn that legal loopholes in every state permitted marriage before kids turned eighteen. In more than half of the U.S., the loopholes were so gaping that they did not specify a minimum age for marriage at all.

Did you know that between 2000 and 2010, the U.S. allowed nearly 250,000 child marriages? Some of these kids were teens like Devon, but I also learned that the majority of those children were minor girls married to adult men (that's nearly 191,000 little girls!). Even more shocking, children as young as twelve were granted marriage licenses in Alaska, Louisiana, and South Carolina.[2] In fact, a nonprofit called Unchained at Last spent a year analyzing marriage license data, revealing that among thirty-seven states that provided data, twenty-two of them allowed marriage for children ages fourteen and younger.[3] In those parts of America, kids have been granted marriage licenses well before they reached the age of sexual consent. How does that make sense?

Back in 2002, Minki and I were twenty-five years old and just recently married, often working through challenges we felt too immature to handle. Devon was only sixteen, and Michael just two years her senior at eighteen. Were they ready for this? I shared my concerns with Minki; financial practicality and the inconvenience of a long drive didn't feel like the best reasons to get married. But my husband reminded me, "We're here to serve a purpose. Our job is to show her unconditional love. And if her parents are all right with it, we certainly aren't in a position to say otherwise."

Both sets of parents were, in fact, supportive of the plan. They even drove up to Cincinnati to sign the necessary paperwork, because in their view, a sooner-than-expected marriage was better than sinfully living together without tying the knot.

— • —

The wedding was going to be family only, a quick affair held at a church in Loveland because the parents had to get back to Kentucky for work on Monday morning. With limited resources, Devon and Michael decided pragmatically to forego a honeymoon, and instead took two days off work to move into their new apartment right after the ceremony. As I helped Devon remove her clothes from the red wardrobe and place them into her suitcase, I stifled my concerns and affixed a bright smile to my face. She chattered excitedly about what they'd need to furnish their apartment, and I promised to help her buy the essentials for her new home.

After Devon moved out, our house felt a little empty, but my husband and I soon established a new routine. We brought two little Boston terriers into our home, or perhaps they could more aptly be referred to as Boston terrors. The big one peed like a wild sprinkler every time he was excited, and the little one lost her mind, barking herself hoarse, every time we had visitors.

One day, the little dogs scrambled to the door, yapping frantically when the doorbell rang. We opened the door, surprised to find our sweet Devon once again standing on the front step. This time, mascara ran in dark rivulets down her face. Her body was racked with silent sobs as one shaking hand lifted a torn piece of notebook paper covered in messy scribble: "You never shut up. I'm done with you." Devon had returned home from the salon that day to find this ripped piece of paper sloppily taped to the front door. In shock, she had pulled her set of keys out of her purse, hoping to find Michael inside. But no matter how hard she tried to unlock the door, her hands, slippery with sweat, struggled to insert the key. She finally fell to her knees on the front porch in defeat, realizing that Michael had changed the locks.

Now, the teenager stood on our porch, unmoving, as I enveloped her in a hug. Suddenly thinking of Lia, I pulled back and examined her face and arms for injuries. Devon realized what I was doing and squeezed my hand. "Oh, Emily, he didn't lay a hand on me," she said. "I don't have any bruises!"

But it soon became clear that she did. Though marks might not have bloomed on her skin's surface, Devon's spirit had been battered and bruised. And this time when she moved back into the room she had just vacated a few months prior, the energy in the house was palpably different. This once energetic, joyful girl who had pulsed with enthusiasm had been replaced by a skittish, downtrodden shadow of her former self. We wondered what could have happened in just a few months to cause such a dramatic change.

Though Devon's circumstances were completely different than Lia's, I experienced an eerie sense of déjà vu. Years ago, I had found one girl with angry bruises swelling on her face. Now, the other limped through each day, nursing scars that only she could see. As I watched the forlorn girl quietly disappear into her room each night after work, a mixture of sadness and rage consumed me. And I experienced the burn of indignation—*this* was my Offense. I realized that I would *never* turn away from bruised, vulnerable children. Like Lia, Devon needed a spare room, a safe place in which to heal, and that was exactly what we were able to provide. However, I often felt unequipped in my attempts to be useful, and in fact, for those first few weeks of her return, I often found myself saying and doing the wrong thing.

I was beside myself with concern, and my type A personality took over as I asked Devon if she wanted to talk. I perched on the foot of her bed and quietly offered to help her find a therapist. With a big smile, I determinedly dragged her to get mani-pedis that weekend. I went on a shopping frenzy and cooked her favorite foods. And then...I stopped. I stopped doing. I realized that none of my actions were helping in the slightest. Many of my reassurances fell on deaf ears, and some of my intended encouragements were even taken as affronts. I soon realized that sometimes, to overcome deep hurt, people don't need us to do a thing. They just need us to be. To be present. To be steady. And particularly challenging for me, to be quiet.

Once we all settled into the silence, like a bird tentatively leaving the security of its nest, Devon began venturing out more frequently for meals instead of taking them in her room. Joining us in the family room in the evenings, she sometimes interrupted the quiet tapping of our fingers on our laptops to share a particularly scary or jarring memory. The more we created a space of quiet acceptance, the more Devon opened up.

—·—

"I called my parents one night. I said that maybe I had made a mistake." The words quietly slipped through Devon's lips one evening. I looked up from my laptop to take in her rigid body seated on the edge of the couch, unblinking eyes trained on the carpet and hands clenched in her lap.

Closing my laptop, I quickly exchanged glances with my husband. We sat in the stillness and listened, only the sound of our breathing rising and falling as Devon spoke. Minki's sharp intake of breath was audible from across the room when we heard how Michael had swerved in traffic, slapping Devon's hand and saying, "Get your hand off the door handle! Don't you trust me?" As his wife fearfully nodded and rubbed the back of her reddening hand, he worked himself into a frenzy.

"My own wife! Holding on to the door handle like she don't trust her own husband! How do you think that makes me feel? What do you have to say for yourself?"

By then, Devon had already learned to quickly apologize. The familiar words tumbled out, tripping over each other in her haste to calm the furious man: "I'm so sorry, honey. I wasn't paying attention. Of *course* I trust you! I trust you with my life! I don't know what came over me. It'll never happen again."

My own breathing soon became irregular as she shakily recalled the phone call with her parents late that night. Her father's stern voice chastised her through the line: "Well, it's just too late. You made your bed, young missy, now you gotta sleep in it. God don't look kindly on divorce, and I'm not having a daughter of mine disgracing the family like that. You do what you gotta do and figure it out." The girl had clutched the phone receiver with both hands, weeping in despair long after the dial tone had gone dead.

The following few weeks blurred together as Devon did her best to "figure it out." She found herself apologizing for smiling when Michael let out a burp. She hastily asked forgiveness for leaving crumbs on the kitchen counter. She drove home half-blinded by tears the day she had foolishly tried to surprise him at the shop and was rudely sent home like a disobedient child, the guys' scornful laughter still echoing in her mind.

A few nights after Devon opened up to us, we held back our own tears as she shared the most horrifying story yet. It marked the day she finally realized that she had allowed herself to become trapped in what felt like an inescapable situation.

One late afternoon when Devon wasn't scheduled at the salon, a neighbor knocked frantically at the door, nearly hyperventilating with anxiety. Her little boy had fallen out of their backyard tree, and she needed to rush him to the emergency room with what looked like a broken arm. Could Devon come over and keep an eye on the baby? It would probably be quick, but the neighbor didn't want to bring the baby girl to the emergency room with her son screaming bloody murder, and she had no idea where her insurance card was.

Of course, the gentle-hearted teenager agreed. Secretly, she was glad for a change of pace in her humdrum life. She had always loved babies, and delightedly picked up the eight-month-old girl as soon as she entered the home. What a darling, sweet thing! Devon gave her a warm bottle, tidied up the kitchen, and even folded some laundry she found haphazardly dumped on the lumpy family room couch.

It was still too early to put the baby down, so Devon decided to take her out for a little stroll. Humming softly to herself, the teen settled the gurgling infant in her stroller, tucked a soft knitted throw around her, and headed out the door. The streetlamps had just turned on, as dusk was settling softly like a warm blanket over the neighborhood. Devon spoke quietly to the baby as she walked: "Do you see that white banana in the sky? It's a skinny-looking little thing. I know it's hard to believe, but that's the moon." Devon had moved on to describing a scattering of pine cones on the ground when the bucolic evening was suddenly interrupted by the piercing scream of police sirens. Alarmed by the loud, sudden noise, the baby began to wail.

Startled out of her quiet monologue, Devon quickly scooped up the baby. She held the squirming infant in her right arm and used her left hand to cover the baby's ears, cradling her head protectively. She stepped off the sidewalk and into the grass, hoping to put some distance between the baby and the oncoming police cars. And then suddenly, the evening exploded in aggressive fury.

The police cars came screeching to a stop in a semicircle around Devon, and an officer shouted emphatically over his PA system: "Devon Jacobsen, put the baby down and keep your hands where we can see them!"

Terrified, Devon froze. She couldn't just put the baby down; the infant was already red-faced and wailing. Her mind whirled as she thought back to that tube of lipstick she might have slipped into her pocket at the drugstore earlier in the week. Body rigid and eyes wide, Devon began to panic.

One of the more compassionate police officers approached her, both hands open in front of his body. He spoke quietly: "It's OK. Just put the baby down. I know she's crying, but she'll be OK. I have two little ones at home...I know." He gently took the baby and returned her to the stroller. Arms suddenly empty, Devon felt naked and exposed. She wrapped her arms around herself and asked, "Sir, what's going on? I'm just taking the baby for a walk! I mean, her mom didn't specifically say I could, but she didn't say I can't! I wasn't *stealing* her!" As she heard her own words, the terror and confusion that had been churning inside overflowed as great hiccupping sobs escaped her strangled chest.

As the other officers stood back, some of them turning off their flashing lights, Devon got ahold of herself. With tears still streaming down her face, she turned to the police officer by the stroller. "OK, I'm OK now. Can you *please* tell me what's going on?"

The large man gently suggested they walk the baby back home, and signaled covertly to the other officers, who one by one began driving away. As the kind officer walked with her, Devon learned that Michael had come home a few hours prior, surprised and angry that she wasn't waiting for him at home.

When he entered the empty house, the young man's mind had begun to race, and he quickly convinced himself that she'd left him. As he imagined his young wife with someone else, a jealous fury began to boil in the pit of his stomach. And because she was only seventeen years old, Michael was able to report Devon as a runaway. That's why the police had turned out as they had, prepared to legally drag an unruly teenager back to her home.

Now in the quiet of our house, Devon relived that awful night, remembering how she had felt like a helpless captive. According to the law, she was old enough to get married but not old enough to leave her spouse. The courts had allowed her to wed, yet she realized they didn't allow her to apply for a divorce or even escape to a domestic violence shelter until she turned eighteen years old. The romantic notions that had filled her imagination with beautiful dreams of family suddenly twisted around her like ugly vines that looked alarmingly like the bars of a cage.

Yet, Devon was one of the lucky ones. She had a support network in our community, and a safe place to stay for as long as she needed. Grown-ups were available to help her navigate rocky terrain with both her husband and her family. And she had remarkable grit, which later drove her to pursue a degree and start fresh.

— · —

I learned so much living with Devon. First, my eyes were opened to the risks associated with the government's allowing child marriage. I applaud lobbyists like Fraidy Reiss, who has made it her life's mission to advocate for a minimum marriage age of eighteen years.

In our houseguest, I also witnessed the resilience of the human spirit. Though we may feel brittle and fragile at times, we are far stronger and more agile than we believe. I also learned a new way to love. I'm a person of action—thinking ahead to a solution, garnering resources, laying out a plan. But with Devon, I learned to extend the gift of *not doing*. She didn't need me to take action on her behalf; she just needed me to be with her. Quiet and personal space were what Devon needed to feel safe and eventually recover from her trauma.

My husband eventually had the excellent idea of sending her to a three-day career camp, which would provide her with the opportunity to explore options and consider what she wanted to do next. When Devon returned from those few days away, an echo of her former self began to permeate the home. Her eyes shone in that familiar way as she talked about becoming an accountant. I personally couldn't fathom her newly discovered love of lining up tidy columns of numbers but was overjoyed to see her passion for life returning. Today, Devon is happily remarried and loves nothing more than a well-balanced spreadsheet.

Finally, in those six months, Minki and I came to a realization about our Offense. After sharing life with the child bride, we recounted our experience and committed to the idea that as a family, we would always open our spare room to abused, neglected, or vulnerable young people.

The Sensation of Choking
Montana, 2013

Shannon stared in horror at the contents of the sea turtle's stomach. Slowly, the striking brunette counted eight plastic bottle caps embedded in the remains of the dead animal's stomach. She listened to the impassioned declaration of the energy policy expert and CEO, Carl—"Millions of sea animals are literally choking on our plastic!"—as the hairs on her arms prickled with gooseflesh. In her mind, she suddenly heard the sweet, plaintive voice of her five-year-old daughter, Ava: "Mom, it feels like there's a plastic cap stuck in my throat."

On November 27, 2013, just three days after she was born, Ava had begun projectile vomiting after every feeding. A day that had dawned in quiet, serene joy had quickly metamorphosed into a seemingly unending nightmare.

Early that morning, in the satiny gray moments just before the sun began to rise, Shannon awoke to quiet gurgling and the soft smacking sounds of her newborn. Rubbing sleep from her eyes and tucking her curly brown hair behind one ear, the new mother smiled adoringly at the squirming bundle lying in the bassinet beside her.

A few moments later, Shannon felt her milk let down as the hungry infant latched on. Blissfully content, mother and daughter lay connected, warm and swaddled in their own private cocoon. But as Shannon gently lifted the baby's head, preparing to switch sides, Ava's blue eyes suddenly popped wide open and a rushing flow of milk spewed from the baby's mouth. The white liquid launched an impossible distance as though propelled from deep within, splattering the wall on the opposite side of the bassinet. Alarmed, Shannon put the baby on her other breast, cradling her with one arm as she clumsily wiped down the wall with the other. Her body wound tight with anxiety, she watched Ava carefully as the baby finished nursing. But apprehension quickly gave way to alarm, as once again the baby's body heaved with violent contractions.

Soon, Ava was vomiting twenty to thirty times a day. Doctors diagnosed acid reflux, seemingly unconcerned as they promised that the baby's digestion would settle down when her system matured. But by the time Ava was two, she had begun doubling over with terrible stomachaches, screaming in pain. Seated next to her daughter on the kitchen floor after an episode, Shannon wiped the tears from Ava's intense blue eyes, even as hot tears spilled from her own. Her jaw clenched tightly in helplessness as her shaking hands sought to soothe her daughter's cramped, writhing body.

Shannon and Ava continued to visit Gastrointestinal Specialists, seeking to solve the mystery of the toddler's physical distress; the weary mom juggled medical appointments with the daily operations of running her marketing agency, Spur Studio, as CEO. She was known as an outstanding storyteller, and her agency was sought after for its innovative campaigns. Yet, despite their tremendous success, Shannon was plagued with restlessness. In her heart, she just knew she could do so much more.

On the rare days she allowed herself to dream, feeling pulled to have a bigger impact in the world, the CEO chastised herself, "The agency's doing great. Our clients trust us, and we're winning awards." She whispered resignedly to herself, "This is as good as it's going to get, and most importantly, we're able to pay all those medical bills."

Spur Studio continued to thrive in 2016. Leaving another successful meeting with her biggest client one afternoon, Shannon got in the car to pick Ava up from preschool. The familiar streets glided by as she turned inward and examined her emotions. Though her client had loved her new campaign ideas, the CEO felt strangely melancholy. Trying to lift herself out of despondency, Shannon shifted her focus to gratitude. "The agency is going strong after four awesome years," she reassured herself. Steady work and a reliable income had afforded a winter season of skiing with her little girl. And just the previous weekend, they'd done some spring cleaning and bought new clothes for the season.

"How blessed we are with this bountiful life!" Shannon proclaimed. But the words fell flat with falseness, and she grimaced. The agency executive sighed deeply, thinking: "I'm doing things that aren't meaningful to me. I help companies sell products and services. Is this really all there is?" Feeling subdued yet still grateful for the work, she thought, "OK, work doesn't have to lift my heart. I don't need to feel fully engaged; *Ava's* the one who needs me engaged." Turning into the school parking lot, she admonished herself: "Just help people sell their stuff and let them pay you already."

— • —

The next few years passed in a haze of doctor visits and medical experiments. Ava grew into a fiercely determined girl, the magical embodiment of squishy joy and spunky lightning. Though she was vomiting constantly, and on some days, couldn't even swallow solid food, the child's piercing blue eyes glinted with mischievous humor. Every few weeks, the kindergartener geared up for another biopsy, endoscopy, or esophageal dilation with a new specialist. Along the way, in order to eliminate all possible food allergies, the five-year-old girl had uncomplainingly accepted a new diet that was free of all wheat, dairy, nuts, soy, eggs, and shellfish.

One sunny Saturday morning, however, Ava succumbed to one of her rare meltdowns. Running into her mom's room and jumping excitedly onto the bed in her favorite flowered dress, the impish girl shouted, "Beach, mama! Let's go to the beach today!" Still under the covers, Shannon turned to gaze affectionately at her daughter, glancing out the window to take in what promised to be a perfect summer Montana day. "Wow, it does look like it's going to be a great beach day, bae. But we're meeting the new specialist today, remember? Let's do that first, then I'll take you to Bozeman Beach after."

Ava's brow furrowed, and the perfect line of freckles that lay across the bridge of her nose scrunched together in displeasure. "No more, mama! Not today, not on a *weekend*!" Shannon reached out to gather that unyielding little body close, inhaling the sweet smell of her silky blond hair as her daughter sobbed in frustration. "I know, I know, love. But this doctor is a specialist who might have some new ideas. Maybe with his help, and you'll even be able to eat a whole ice cream cone at the beach." At the singsong lilt in her mom's voice, Ava looked up hopefully, still sniffling. One large tear gathered on the tip of her upturned nose as she asked, "Really, mom? Do you think I could?"

One breakfast and three bouts of vomiting later, mother and daughter were seated in yet another exam room. Ava glanced up at the smiling giraffe painted on the wall, imagining the animal turning away from the sharp antiseptic smell that permeated the room. She did everything the man in the white coat asked, all the same things she had done a hundred times before. Then, as the consultation drew to a close, Shannon's body tensed with expectation as the specialist proclaimed, "Well, I know what we need to do to help Ava." Her heart rate accelerating, Shannon reached for her daughter's small hand. Would the mystery of Ava's medical condition finally be resolved?

But five short minutes later, the incensed mother scooped her daughter up and hastily backed through the door, one arm wrapped protectively around the girl. Glaring at the doctor with a mixture of outrage and disappointment, she stormed out of the office without another word.

Strapped safely back in the car, Ava hesitantly asked, "Mama, what's a feeding tube?" The five-year-old had heard the surgeon's cavalier words as he'd suggested removing a portion of her esophagus. When he declared "this would change her life forever," Shannon had sat stunned when she realized the man was referring to a lifelong need for a feeding tube, not freedom from the endless vomiting.

Later that afternoon, Shannon donned oversized sunglasses and lay in the warm sand as she watched Ava splashing in the water. She finally allowed the tears to flow behind the dark lenses, as her daughter waved cheerfully from the water's edge.

Earlier, just three licks into her ice cream cone, Ava had dropped the dessert in agony as she retched into the public trash can. Now, Shannon looked back on years of endless medical visits, each snapshot like a disappointing half-developed Polaroid. She felt as if a fist were mercilessly squeezing her heart, crushing the tender flesh. Reclining in the warm sand on that perfect day, Shannon felt anxiety pressing in on her from every angle, her life folding in on itself and contracting with dizzying force.

Then, Carl called. Though it had been a few years since Shannon had done public relations work with the energy policy expert, she instantly recognized the warm, animated voice that projected from her phone. She remembered the CEO as a visionary who got excited about solving the world's big problems with solutions like infrastructure development and grid innovation. The two agreed to meet for lunch later that week, and Shannon looked forward to reconnecting with someone who passionately loved his work. "Maybe a little of his zeal will rub off on me," she thought ruefully.

"Millions of sea animals are choking on our plastic!" Carl asserted earnestly. "We are literally *drowning* in our waste. Like most Americans, you may think we are recycling our plastic. But in reality, we're spending tons of money to ship it out to other countries—where it's getting burned or dumped in rivers."

Shannon listened, dumbfounded. All those plastics she'd carefully rinsed and deposited in the blue bin were...being burned in Third World countries? Gesturing animatedly with his fork, the forgotten meal cooling on his plate, Carl continued. Less than 10 percent of all plastics were recycled, and the rest were incinerated or left floating in the ocean. And now he had a way to remove ocean plastics from the waste stream permanently. In fact, his technology was able to eliminate up to five tons of plastic a day. He was founding a new organization and wanted her to be his Executive Director.

The marketer was mulling over the unexpected offer when Carl's next words hit her like an ice-cold ocean wave: "Can you imagine what it feels like to choke to death on plastic, Shannon? I need someone to help me tell this story."

Yes, she knew *exactly* what that was like. Shannon's brain buzzed with the shocking data, as unfamiliar phrases like "plasma arc technology" and images of tiny, red-faced Ava heaving painfully whirled in her mind like waves crashing over one another. Shannon drew the lunch to an early close, as she felt her worlds colliding. Shaking Carl's hand, she promised to thoughtfully consider the offer.

That evening, Ava insisted on sleeping in her favorite white faux-fur coat. Reading the determined set of her daughter's chin and eager to read up on ocean plastics, Shannon conceded. So, the little girl flashed her mother one last triumphant smile before snuggling into her soft flannel sheets, looking like she was ready for an all-night rave in her rainbow-striped leggings and dark chipped nail polish. After leaving the door open just a crack, Shannon padded to the kitchen. She poured herself a glass of pinot and flipped open her laptop, settling into her favorite spot at the table.

It was well past midnight when Shannon finally shut down her computer, running her fingers through her hair and stretching. She had found overwhelming evidence that Carl's data was accurate. Not only was 91 percent of plastic not being recycled, but 79 percent was being discarded in landfills and the ocean.[4] Shannon learned that 2018 had been a pivotal year, when China stopped accepting waste from the United States and instituted what it called the National Sword policy. For decades up until then, because China had needed materials for its manufacturing industry, the country had recycled nearly half of the world's waste. But because so much of that waste was contaminated by nonrecyclable materials, an estimated 1.3 to 1.5 million metric tons of plastic was ending up on China's coasts each year.[5]

As a result of China's policy change, the U.S. was now sending plastic waste to developing countries with cheap labor and less defined environmental rules, such as Cambodia, Bangladesh, and Ethiopia.[6] Not only were local populations suffering from respiratory illnesses caused by the toxic fumes when they incinerated the waste, but more and more of that waste was ending up in the ocean each year. "This is more than despicable," Shannon thought. "It's downright *offensive*." Suddenly, the heartbreaking frustration of Ava's undiagnosed condition flooded through her. Just as her little girl choked and fought for her breath, the world was choking on plastic waste. Burning with indignation, Shannon realized: "This is what I am meant to do."

The next morning, after two vomiting spells, Shannon dropped Ava off at kindergarten. Threading her way to the downtown office of SeaChange, she felt her pulse quicken with excitement. While she still found the science intimidating, the marketer also realized that this job provided the perfect opportunity for her to leverage her skills for meaningful impact. With SeaChange in start-up mode, Shannon could envision how her strategic thinking and planning skills would contribute to the organization. And though she had much to learn, Shannon believed her storytelling skills could be put to work in a new way.

"I've never thought of the plasma arc as a 'contained lightning bolt,' but that's an excellent way to describe it," Carl said, turning the concept over in his mind. Just a few weeks after their initial meeting, they were now laying out the SeaChange launch plan after Shannon had made the tough decision to close up her agency. Through that transition period, she flip-flopped between pure exhilaration and stomach-churning anxiety. On a few occasions, the world felt like it suddenly had tilted precariously as Shannon considered the dramatic pivot she was making in her career and life. But in short order, the marketing executive would feel herself return to solid footing, confident in the knowledge that this was the right move. Shannon had identified her Offense; the waste that choked marine animals and damaged our oceans had struck a resonant chord within her.

So, over the next few weeks, she ingested masses of complex data, transforming them into simple, digestible infographics. Within a few months, Shannon had helped develop the organization's narrative. She immensely enjoyed the electrifying sizzle of neurons firing as she grappled with the complex science and leveraged her skills to contribute to the worthwhile mission.

Six months into her new job and rejuvenated with positivity, Shannon decided to treat Ava with a ticket to *The Nutcracker* ballet. But on the winter morning of the performance, endless bouts of vomiting foreshadowed a difficult day ahead. A few hours later, fatigued and dehydrated, the little girl fell asleep at the ballet, cottony wisps of hair drifting over her face as her head rested wearily against her mother's shoulder. Later, when the audience filed out of the theater, Ava wept in frustration, tears coursing down her face. "Why can't I be normal?" she lamented. "All the other kids are going out for cocoa, and I can't even *swallow* it!"

That evening, Shannon desperately reached out to her entire network, seeking new medical counsel. Her six-year-old's health was failing and she weighed just thirty-five pounds, but the beleaguered mother was determined to find answers. She soon connected with Boston Children's Hospital.

Within a month, mother and daughter had relocated to Boston for weekly appointments. Discovering that the girl's esophagus had constricted to just three millimeters versus a normal diameter of ten to fifteen millimeters, her new doctor began biweekly dilations that significantly reduced Ava's nausea. Today, Shannon continues to work remotely for SeaChange, as Ava prepares for a laparoscopic procedure that will set her up for continued long-term improvement.

The idea of surgery frightens Ava, but like her mother, she is facing the future with renewed strength. Learning that sea turtles were choking on plastic, she had exclaimed with a spark of recognition, "I know *exactly* how that feels!" The compassionate duo, intimately familiar with what humans are doing to wildlife and developing nations, is determined to both resolve Ava's medical issues and help the millions of animals being choked to death in the ocean.

SeaChange has planned its first mission for the winter of 2021 to 2022; it will be to Indonesia, where 1.5 million tons of plastic are entering the ocean each year. Wrestling down staggering personal challenges and rising with renewed purpose, Shannon is now passionately living out her social legacy.

The Other Side
Minnesota, 2002

"I am a fast runner because a hippopotamus trained me," Abdo stated with a playful gleam in his eye.

Harper, a blond, ponytailed college freshman, stared with amused curiosity at her friend as they walked side by side. "What do you mean, you were trained by a hippo?" she asked.

The tall, gentle man led his friend to a nearby bench. Speaking in his deep, melodic voice, Abdo relived one of his most terrifying childhood memories. "We had no shoes. The bottoms of our feet were torn open and bleeding. Our stomachs growled ferociously with hunger, and our group of boys had walked hundreds of miles, often going days without food and drinking dirty water. We were terrified, exhausted, and very weak. And that was when we met the hippo."

Harper listened in stunned silence, as she realized her track teammate had been one of the more than twenty thousand children UNICEF called "the lost boys."[7] At just seven years old, he was one of the kids who witnessed their homes being attacked by the Sudan People's Liberation Army. These boys witnessed their fathers being slaughtered and their sisters and mothers raped or dragged away by the soldiers.

On the day his village was attacked, Abdo's brother grabbed his hand; together they ran away from the devastating hell that had once been their home. Over the next few weeks, they came across hundreds of newly orphaned boys, some carrying weapons they didn't know how to use, others carrying infants they didn't know how to feed.

A month into their seemingly endless journey, Abdo had already watched many of his friends succumb to starvation and disease. One evening as he and his brother settled down to sleep, the boy wearily threw his arm around his brother's bony shoulders, saying, "We will survive. I shall care for you, and you shall care for me."

Harper listened, spellbound, as her friend remembered waking later that night to a sky lit with brightly twinkling stars. He left his sleeping brother nestled in the base of a tree, to relieve himself. A few minutes later, Abdo screamed just one word, *"Climb!"* as he sprinted to the nearest tree and frantically clambered up as high as he could, a furious hippo charging after him. He reported to Harper, with a faraway look in his eyes, that no one died that evening. "And today," the young man continued, "when I feel I cannot continue with our drills, I imagine that hippo behind me and find I can run just a little bit further after all!"

Harper sat quietly, absorbing the incredible stories she'd heard from her teammate, so foreign and unfamiliar on this bright spring day in Minneapolis. Abdo had walked hundreds of grueling miles as a little boy and lived in a refugee camp for years before coming to America. The clean-cut face to which she had grown so accustomed now seemed to come from another universe entirely. And having grown up in a tight-knit midwestern community, the college freshman suddenly realized how insular her childhood had been. Abdo's story catalyzed a thirst to expand her world. Overtaken by curiosity and indignation, she wondered, "How could a seven-year-old become orphaned and displaced, all in one day?" That afternoon, she thought determinedly, "I want to hear about what's going on in places like Sudan from different voices like Abdo's. If I really care about the world we live in, I need to experience the other side."

— · —

When the spirited twenty-two-year-old completed university a few years later, she remembered that moment sitting on the bench with her friend and, fueled by a desire to understand the situation of displaced people, Harper actively pursued an opportunity to live on "the other side." She made a bold move to accept her first job in the Democratic Republic of Congo, where, signing on with a nonprofit called HEAL Africa, her responsibilities involved bridging local field operations with the organization's American investors. And as one of just a handful of non-Congolese people on the two-hundred-person staff, the blond, blue-eyed young woman certainly stood out as she sought to understand and then paint a picture of daily life for those back at home. Though she spoke neither Swahili nor French, Harper dove right into her job, learning two new languages and meeting hundreds of patients and their families.

One morning at the medical facility, a sweet voice singing "Ave Maria" drew Harper into one of the treatment rooms. The beautiful song pierced her heart; it was something achingly familiar in her new, foreign world. And as she entered the room, Harper was drawn to a mesmerizing nine-year-old girl seated between two physical therapists. The small head of the child, Kavine, waved left and right to music only she could hear as she continued to sing, her dark eyes fixed on the older woman seated across from her.

Harper learned that Kavine's birth had been difficult and, from her first breath, it had been apparent that the child had been born with a number of congenital diseases. Just a few weeks later, her grief-stricken grandmother took in Kavine when both of the baby girl's parents were murdered. Repurposing an old shirt, the elderly lady fashioned a sling that she then altered every few years to accommodate the growing girl. For the next nine years, she carried Kavine everywhere. Now, though the long-limbed child hung awkwardly on her grandma's back, the elderly lady had carried her grandbaby more than 250 miles through rural Congo to seek treatment at HEAL Africa Hospital.

With the soulful melody still echoing behind her, Harper stepped out of the room and returned to her morning routine. Through Kavine's story, she had just glimpsed the extraordinary sacrifice patients made to journey to the hospital. Harper became determined to help every patient who arrived at the hospital, though all 150 beds were full and hundreds of sick and hurting people spilled into the hallways. When a dusty soccer ball bounced hard against her shin, the athletic American was jolted out of her musings and looked up. Then she enthusiastically joined a group of young patients for a quick game of soccer in the courtyard.

A few moments later, still breathing heavily, she gladly accepted a bottle of cold water from an English-speaking coworker. Harper asked, "How long are those kids going to be here? I've seen them every day since I arrived." The Congolese nurse responded, "The children are often here for many months. Some are awaiting their own medical procedures. Others have accompanied their parents, who are being treated at the hospital."

"But what about school?" the American asked. "They're going to fall behind if they're out of class for so long!"

Harper's revelation soon translated into action. Just a few weeks into her new life at the hospital, the college graduate already appreciated the entrepreneurial spirit that flowed through her organization. When a need was identified, there was no real chain of command to gain approval. All the workers did their best to scrape together resources and resolve the myriad issues they came across each day. Going with the flow, Harper asked around in halting Swahili and found good-hearted teachers willing to engage the children. Then she collected educational materials and identified a block of free space. Within a month, the now twenty-three-year-old had claimed the space, assembled a classroom, and established herself as the principal of her own school.

Harper had just celebrated her one-year anniversary with HEAL Africa when it finally happened. The American succumbed to malaria and ended up as a patient in one of her own hospital beds. Feverish and uncomfortable, the young woman awoke from a particularly puzzling dream three days into her illness. Not one to idolize celebrities or swoon over Hollywood actors, she couldn't understand why she had dreamt that Ben Affleck was visiting her.

Though Harper was groggy and ill for their first meeting, she quickly realized that Ben had in fact been visiting the hospital while she was sick. The two soon developed a relationship grounded in a common passion for supporting the people of eastern Congo. And one year later, when Ben cofounded the Eastern Congo Initiative (ECI), Harper became one of his first employees. She was proud to join an organization that takes a somewhat novel view of philanthropy, which resonated with all she had seen and learned in the field. Rather than fundraising for short-term relief efforts, as so many nonprofits do, ECI seeks to fund Congolese-led programs, investing in local, community-based initiatives for sustainable development and growth.

— • —

Already outside her American safety net, Harper once again found herself on the other side of her comfort zone. With HEAL Africa, she had learned the nuances of hospital operations with a robust community of like-minded people, quickly picking up new languages and capabilities. But now, as the first ECI employee in Congo, she was all alone in the field.

Independently, the now twenty-five-year-old learned to assess local nonprofits and build a competitive landscape. She researched how to legally incorporate the organization, and wrote grant proposals. Fully employing the entrepreneurial skills she had picked up at HEAL Africa, Harper helped ECI extend its first grants just seven months after starting her new job. She felt a gratifying sense of fulfillment in seeing those grants go to former child soldiers, furnishing them with vocational training that would lead to stable jobs and a secure future.

Over the next seven years, Harper found her work with ECI enormously rewarding, though she often missed the comforts of American living. One Friday evening, she headed back to her apartment in the dusty heat, anticipating a long shower after having gained approval for her three-pronged strategy for the coming year. As she entered her home at the base of beautiful Lake Kivu, in the city of Goma, Harper flipped the light switch and sighed. The power had gone out again. This meant, to wash away the day's grime, she would have to warm water on her gas stove, mix it with cool water in a bucket, and pour it over her head as a makeshift shower. Still, as she glanced out the window, she counted herself among the lucky ones with access to plumbing. Every morning, she watched countless neighbors trudge to the lake with yellow jerry cans, filling them with water for the day.

The next morning, Harper watched the bobbing dots of yellow as the daily trek for water began. She was overcome by a sudden craving for the familiar flavors of home. "What I wouldn't give for a good cup of coffee!" she thought.

Possessed by a sudden zeal to find the best coffee in Goma, Harper rode all over town that weekend, speaking to shopkeepers and even farmers. She returned home Sunday evening, legs weary from cycling and stomach burning with too many cups of bitter coffee. She faced the surprising reality: though agriculture was the main source of income in eastern Congo, farmers were selling their hard-earned crops to middlemen, who sold to other middlemen, and so on all the way up a highly profitable chain. Ultimately, all the good coffee left the country, and the farmers received next to nothing for their back-breaking labor.

That's when ECI began its coffee and cocoa work in earnest. Other nonprofits cautioned Harper about the long lead times required to invest in long-term crops, compared to the more immediate relief that could be realized from handing out seeds and tools. But approaching the opportunity with the same dedication as she had for her HEAL Africa school years ago, Harper persisted. Now, after nearly a decade of working in Africa, she understood how to navigate the local infrastructure, organizing 4,500 farmers who had been selling independently. She financed cooperatives, convinced the government to reduce export tax, and ultimately sold the cooperatives' coffee to giant retailers like Starbucks. In fact, this ECI initiative soon changed the entire Congolese coffee industry. Farmers tripled their income from coffee, and proudly repaid 100 percent of their loans in the process.

While wins like this were tremendously rewarding, living "on the other side" wasn't always easy for Harper. Goma, which sits on the border of Congo and Rwanda and is the capital city of North Kivu province, was considered an active conflict zone at the time. And in November 2012, the famous M23 rebellion descended upon the capital. A rebel military group took control of Harper's town, forcing 140,000 people to flee their homes.[8] As the city was bombed, many fled to HEAL Africa Hospital. Others simply took cover, praying that the interminable whistling bombs would not demolish their homes.

In the midst of the violence, Harper considered fleeing Congo for America, but she found herself unable to leave her friends. One young lady she worked with, Rosa, weighed particularly heavily on her mind. Two years ago, Rosa had married a man who abused her. The mistreatment had escalated, and Harper knew the terrified girl had been planning to run away the same weekend of the rebellion. What would she do now? How would she choose between the horrors in her home and the nightmare outside?

Harper received a quick text from her friend later that same day: "Leaving tonight for Rwanda. Pray I don't get caught! Love, your soon-to-be refugee friend, Rosa." The women lost touch after the rebellion, but Harper saved the text, reading and rereading the few words.

"A refugee among refugees," she thought. Previously, neighbors had filled her in on the devastating impact of the volcano that had erupted in 2002 and wiped out the entire town of Goma. All one million inhabitants had fled, returned, and rebuilt. In fact, everyone Harper met in the town had once been a refugee. And as soon as Rosa crossed the border into Rwanda, she would be considered a refugee, too. Years ago, Harper's track teammate Abdo in Minneapolis had been labeled a refugee first in Kenya, and later in America.

Now, ten years after hearing his story in college, Harper remembered her desire to experience the various angles of current events. And the past decade had indeed revealed a very different perspective on displaced people and poverty. She had developed lifelong friendships, learned two new languages, worked for Ben Affleck, and met countless celebrities, journalists, and business leaders. And in yet another unexpected turn, Harper had now been offered her next new job. When her recent success in operationalizing the Congolese coffee industry gained the attention of executives at the Starbucks Corporation, she was offered a prestigious role as Director of Global Coffee Strategy in Seattle.

Seeking to experience and understand the other side had provided Harper with previously unimagined opportunities. So, in April 2016, the American woman who had lived her entire adult life in eastern Congo moved back to the United States, her luggage filled with fragrant packages of Starbucks Reserve Congolese coffee, and with Kavine's haunting melody floating through her mind.

Today, Harper leads global coffee and cocoa supply chain sustainability at Starbucks. At home, she effortlessly transitions from English to Swahili as she converses with her African nanny. She and her partner have surrounded their baby boy, Elijah, with books, culture, and friends from all over the world. For Elijah, Harper is working to build a world where there will be no "other side."

—REFLECTION—

In the course of our daily lives, we encounter multiple injustices that distress us. But for each of us, there's one Offense that stands out among the others. It's the thing that tugs uncomfortably at our gut and pesters our conscience until we take action. For my family, as you know by now, it's abused, neglected, or vulnerable children. Years ago, at just twenty-two years old, Harper sought to put a face on poverty and appreciate firsthand the experiences of displaced people. And in Shannon's case, she has named her Offense in how humans are polluting our world and unwittingly killing millions of animals.

At the end of Chapter One, you had the opportunity to define your unique Offer. Now, as you finish reading Chapter Two, take some time to try and put a name on your Offense, that injustice that you find most egregious. First we looked inward, and now let's take a look outward.

As I considered the best way to frame up a holistic view of potential Offenses, the United Nations' seventeen Sustainable Development Goals (see Figure 2.1, p. 84) seemed to provide a good framework, because they cover everything from social and economic issues to environmental issues.

So, let's dive in. Please read through the statements in Figure 2.2, which bring each issue to life with tangible, real-world examples. Because some of us may feel more compelled to safeguard our familiar and immediate environment, while others may be most affected by a broader impact on our nation or the globe, you will find descriptions that range from your most personal space to the wider nation and the world.

Do consider your reaction as you read through them. Some lines may resonate: "Yes, that's always been something that has bothered me." Others may bring back a memory from the past: "I used to be involved in that." Place a check in the box next to the statements that stand out for you.

Figure 2.1 (Source: un.org)

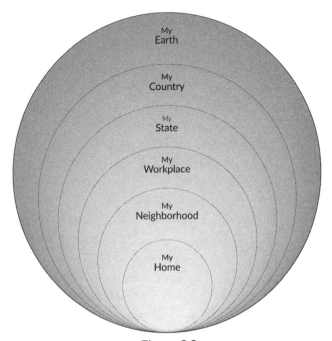

Figure 2.2

1. No Poverty

a. According to the 2018 census, one in six American children lives in poverty.[9] These vulnerable kids are at a greater risk of dropping out of school and experiencing abuse and neglect.[10]

☐ *I want to help kids in the United States escape abusive situations and stay in school.*

b. In low- and middle-income countries around the world, 385 million children live on less than $1.90 per day[11] and 8,500 children die every day due to poor nutrition.[12]

☐ *I want to help children around the world rise out of extreme poverty.*

c. Women and single moms are disproportionately impacted by poverty.[13] Many don't have access to money, are trapped in situations of domestic violence, and are isolated from social support networks.

☐ *I want to help abused women transition into a safe, stable life situation.*

Walk in their shoes. Every year, our family initiates a deprivation practice. We choose something to go without for a set period of time, to remind ourselves not to take our abundance for granted. Interested? Here are some ideas. (Yes, we've done them all!)

· *Eat only rice and beans for a week.*

· *No grocery shopping for a month; eat only what's in the pantry, fridge, and freezer. (Yes, there's really more than enough there!)*

· *No snacks for a month, just three meals a day.*

· *No coffee runs; brew only at home.*

2. Zero Hunger

a. More than thirty-seven million people in the United States struggle with hunger, including more than eleven million children.[14] For these children, school lunch is often the last healthy meal they consume for the day.[15]

□ *I want to feed America's hungry children.*

b. After a decade of progress, global hunger has been on the rise these past three years. According to the UN, one in nine people worldwide has suffered from hunger[16] and 238 million children younger than five years old are stunted, wasting, or overweight due to poor nutrition.[17]

□ *I want to help the two billion people who are food-insecure by transforming agriculture, influencing public policy, or volunteering to work directly with those who need help.*

3. Good Health and Well-Being

a. In 2017, drug overdose became the leading injury-related death in the United States. Of those deaths, nearly 70 percent involved a prescription or illicit opioid and currently, roughly 130 Americans die every single day as a result of the opioid crisis.[18]

□ *I want to educate families and help my community manage drug-related public health threats.*

b. Approximately one in ten Americans over the age of sixty has experienced some form of elder abuse[19] and globally, the World Health Organization estimates that the numbers are even more extreme: one in six.[20] While the National Center on Elder Abuse indicates that family members are most likely to commit elder abuse, cases of mistreatment have also been identified at institutions like nursing homes and long-term care facilities.

☐ *I would like to care for the elderly in my community by volunteering at an assisted living facility or by visiting or delivering food to seniors living at home.*

☐ *I want to advocate for elders worldwide in long-term care.*

c. Half the world lacks access to essential health services, which in 2018 resulted in 8.6 million preventable deaths in low- and middle-income countries.[21]

☐ *I want to dramatically increase global access to healthcare.*

4. Quality Education

a. According to the National Center for Education Statistics, one in five U.S. adults has low literacy skills.[22] That's forty-three million people. Whether they are among the one in every six teenagers who drop out of high school each year,[23] or among the one million immigrants who come to the United States each year lacking high school education and proficient English skills, these adults read below a fifth-grade level and struggle to earn a living wage, secure stable housing, and know their rights.

> **What if the world really were a village?**
>
> What if we were all held responsible for one another?
>
> What if what happened to one of us impacted all of us?

☐ *I want to improve literacy rates in America.*

☐ *I want to improve global literacy.*

b. Large gender gaps exist in the ability to access education; in fact, girls are four times more likely to be out of school than boys, and sixteen million girls will never set foot in a classroom.[24]

☐ *I want to close the gender gap in education, providing girls everywhere with equal access to education.*

5. Gender Equality

a. Sex trafficking is a form of modern-day slavery and makes up nearly 80 percent of all human trafficking, in which victims are forced, tricked, or coerced into performing commercial sex acts. While victims include all gender identities, an estimated 71 percent of the twenty to forty million enslaved people worldwide are women and girls.[25] And while this may sound like a developing-world issue, the United States is not immune; the U.S. State Department estimates that six hundred thousand to eight hundred thousand slaves are trafficked into America each year.[26]

☐ *I want to end modern-day slavery and help victims who have been rescued from sexual exploitation and trafficking.*
☐ *I want to stop sex trafficking in the United States.*

b. According to UNICEF, each year twelve million girls are married before they turn eighteen,[27] which often ends their education and puts them at greater risk of too-early pregnancy, sexual violence, and domestic abuse. These girls become dependent on their husbands, often without access to their own finances or social support system. Again, this is not a developing-world issue; it's estimated that between 2000 and 2010, nearly 250,000 American children as young as twelve years old were married.

☐ *I want to end child marriage around the world and support women who have escaped forced child marriage.*
☐ *I want to end child marriage in America.*

c. Female genital mutilation (FGM) is a type of gender-based violence that intentionally alters or injures female genitals for nonmedical reasons. This cutting results in extreme pain, and victims face a lifetime of challenges related to their sexual, reproductive, and mental health. In 2020 alone, over four million girls are at risk of undergoing FGM.[28]

☐ *I want to end female genital cutting around the world and support women who have experienced FGM.*

6. Clean Water and Sanitation

a. One in three people globally lacks access to clean drinking water, and more than half of the world lacks access to safe sanitation.[29] That's 2.2 billion people who don't have readily available, contamination-free water and who risk diarrhea, cholera, and death every time they have a drink.

☐ *I want to provide everyone in the world with access to clean water.*

b. Our freshwater ecosystems supply precious drinking water, irrigation, and energy for agriculture, and a home for some of Earth's richest biodiversity. Today, 80 percent of wastewater goes untreated, and demand for fresh water is outstripping supply.[30]

☐ *I feel compelled to protect the world's freshwater supply, improving water-use efficiency and management and upgrading water infrastructure.*

7. Affordable and Clean Energy

a. Renewable energy is clean energy derived from natural resources like the sun, wind, and water; using it can have lasting positive effects on the climate and environment.[31] Unlike nonrenewable sources such as oil and fossil fuels (referred to as "dirty energy"), which are finite and release harmful emissions into our environment, renewable energy is inexhaustible.

> ☐ *I will learn about home renewable energy systems and commit to implement what I can, reducing my consumption of dirty energy and contributing to a brighter future.*

b. While the world has made progress on renewable energy in recent years, 860 million people across the world still live without access to electricity, predominantly in Sub-Saharan Africa,[32] where fewer than a third of health facilities have access to reliable electricity.

> ☐ *I want to break the cycle of poverty by bringing energy to those who don't have it.*

8. Decent Work and Economic Growth

a. Women in the U.S. receive more college and graduate degrees than men and make up nearly half of the workforce. Yet, according to data from the latest census, they earn eighty-two cents for every dollar earned by men, and mothers are paid sixty-nine cents for every dollar paid to fathers.[33]

> ☐ *I want to advocate for equal pay and close the gender wage gap in America.*

b. Globally, 152 million children between the ages of five and seventeen are deprived of access to education and suffer as victims of child labor. And over seventy million kids work in a hazardous environment, exposed to dangerous conditions like open-pit mines, extreme heat, and toxicity.[34]

☐ *I want to fight to stop the exploitation of children.*
☐ *I will become a more conscientious consumer and not perpetuate child labor.*

9. Industry, Innovation, and Infrastructure

a. "Infrastructure" refers to systems that enable basic societal needs to be met; it includes public services like communications, transportation, and education, which are critical to improving community productivity. According to a 2018 UN report that tracked data from 227 cities, only 53 percent of urban residents have convenient access to public transportation,[35] which prohibits access to education and healthcare, and impedes trade, which limits the ability to generate regular income.

☐ *I want to enable global transport solutions like roads, railways, tunnels, and airports where they are needed most.*

b. Innovation enables new skill development, and access to the world's information is a critical enabler. However, in a world where information is power, more than three billion people are still offline,[36] and in the past few years, the global digital gender gap has also widened.[37]

☐ *I want to help equalize the information playing field and provide every person in the world with access to the internet.*

10. Reduced Inequalities

a. Nearly ten thousand children a day are orphaned as a result of wars and conflicts, epidemics, and famine.[38] Further, in many countries, children with disabilities are often discarded; in Central and Eastern Europe, children are forty-five times more likely to be in an orphanage if they are disabled. But the issue is not exclusive to developing regions; over 440,000 children are living in the U.S. foster care system. Per the U.S. Department of Health and Human Services, nearly 125,000 of them are eligible for adoption, while nearly eighteen thousand children age out of the system annually.[39]

> ☐ *I want to provide a better future for orphans around the world, supplying their basic life needs and helping them find forever homes.*
> ☐ *I will consider fostering or adopting an American child who needs a home.*

b. Fifteen percent of the world's population, or one billion people, live with a disability.[40] Notably, 80 percent of those people live in developing countries, where they are less likely to access educational resources, healthcare, or support services. Furthermore, research shows they are more vulnerable to abuse, violence, and marginalization, with less ability to obtain police or legal intervention.[41]

> ☐ *I want to build an inclusive, accessible, and sustainable community for all individuals with disabilities.*

11. Sustainable Cities and Communities

a. Half of today's population now lives in cities, but rapid urbanization is overburdening infrastructure and worsening air pollution. Health and safety hazards are particularly dire for the 883 million people living in slums, those areas lacking clean water, sanitation, and durable housing.[42]

☐ *I want to help establish inclusive, safe, and sustainable urban settlements.*

b. In the United States, more than half a million people are homeless on a single night, with 65 percent seeking refuge in a shelter and 35 percent sleeping unsheltered.[43] A key driver of homelessness is referred to as the "affordability gap," the difference between minimum wage and housing cost. With federal minimum wage held at $7.25 an hour, a minimum-wage worker needs to labor for 122 hours a week to afford a median two-bedroom apartment.[44]

> *What if you were to live forever?*
>
> *What if you weren't going to die, and you were to spend infinity on this earth?*
>
> *How might you change the way you consume or invest in resources?*

☐ *I want to help the homeless transition into permanent housing by providing assistance with job search, childcare, or shelter solutions.*
☐ *I want to lobby for affordable housing.*

12. Responsible Consumption and Production

a. Today, the world produces enough food to feed everyone on the planet, yet 30 to 40 percent of all food is wasted. A key driver of this inefficiency on the production side is the lack of infrastructure, such as cold storage and transport, while on the consumption side, many people lack the purchasing power to access nutritious food. Meanwhile, higher-income countries have an excess of affordable food, wasting 1.3 billion tons of food each year, which could feed as many as two billion people.[45]

☐ *I am committed to minimizing food waste, starting with my own habits.*

☐ *I am interested in food recovery initiatives to distribute unused food to those who need it.*

b. We must balance consumption of constrained resources with sustainable production for the future, which means reducing the raw materials we consume. For instance, phosphorus allows living cells to transfer energy, which ensures soil fertility and maintains high levels of crop yield. Yet its current mismanagement means the planet may run out of this crucial element in just a few decades.[46] Another underappreciated natural commodity is river sand, which is used to make everything from concrete and glass to silicon chips. Fifty billion tons are used each year, making it the world's second-most-consumed natural resource, exceeding even fossil fuels. Exacerbating the issue of consumption exceeding natural renewal, much of the sand trade is undocumented and unregulated, resulting in hundreds killed in battle in the past decade and deltas laid to waste.[47]

☐ *I want to better understand our endangered resources and fight for their management, regulation, and tracking.*

13. Climate Action

Global emissions of greenhouse gases, such as carbon dioxide, have increased nearly 50 percent since 1990,[48] contributing to global warming. As a result, extreme heat waves are negatively impacting agriculture, and melting sea ice and glaciers are causing sea levels to rise. In fact, for every degree the planet warms up, food production falls by 10 to 15 percent.[49]

☐ *I commit to doing my part for climate action by learning about and reducing my carbon footprint.*

14. Life Below Water

The ocean provides more than half the world's oxygen and absorbs 30 percent of human-produced carbon dioxide, buffering the impacts of global warming.[50] But the five trillion pieces of plastic waste in the world's oceans[51] are affecting over eight hundred species of marine animals, which are eating the plastic and dying.[52]

☐ *I want to get involved with protecting and cleaning up our oceans.*

☐ *I will educate myself on what's really being recycled and dramatically curb my plastic consumption.*

15. Life on Land

a. Forests are critical in sustaining life on Earth, supporting more than 80 percent of all terrestrial animals, plants, and insects.[53] Like oceans, forests act as a carbon sponge, soaking up carbon dioxide that would otherwise exacerbate climate change. Yet, while goals were set to reduce deforestation, tree loss actually increased by 43 percent globally between 2001 and 2013[54] due to agricultural demands and illegal logging.[55]

☐ *I will exercise conscientiousness as a consumer to do my part against deforestation.*

☐ *I will fight deforestation by lobbying, fundraising, and raising awareness.*

b. One million animal and plant species are under threat of extinction due to climate change and habitat destruction.[56] In fact, today's loss of species is estimated to be at least one thousand times higher than the natural extinction rate.[57]

☐ *I will protect animals and plants from the threat of extinction to preserve Earth's biodiversity.*

☐ *I will change my lifestyle to minimize the negative impact to wildlife.*

c. While the UN has not included animal cruelty in the Sustainable Development Goals, animal welfare is a topic close to our family's heart. Livestock and horses frequently fall victim to the pervasive animal abuse in the farm industry, and few policies or protections have been put in place to prevent it. Dogs and cats are also common victims of intentional cruelty, hoarding, and neglect. The ASPCA estimates that in the U.S., 6.5 million companion animals enter shelters, and 1.5 million are euthanized every year.[58]

☐ *I want to stop animal cruelty and advocate for those who have no voice.*

☐ *I want to care for or adopt animals in a shelter near me.*

16. Peace, Justice, and Strong Institutions

a. The Universal Declaration of Human Rights states that "all human beings are born free and equal in dignity and rights,"[59] yet the world must increase the pace of establishing national institutions to ensure that those human rights are maintained. These institutions are internationally recognized as effective in implementing human rights standards at a national level, but as of 2019, only 39 percent of all countries had achieved compliance.[60]

☐ *I will take a stand for human rights and fight for a fairer world.*

> *Peace isn't the same as conflict avoidance.*
>
> *We sometimes need conflict to get to a resolution.*
>
> *Do you feel equipped or prepared to face conflict?*

b. Having lived in self-quarantine for the past three months, I am writing this book in the midst of the COVID-19 pandemic, when I can't help but envision millions of us sitting at home, finally forced to come face-to-face with the systemic issues of brutality and prejudice in the United States. Today, though Black Americans make up only 13 percent of the U.S. population, they are two and a half times as likely as white Americans to be killed by the police.[61]

☐ *I want to fight police brutality and stop systemic racism against Black Americans.*

c. Sixty percent of young people have witnessed online bullying,[62] and the majority of them say it affects their ability to learn and feel safe at school. Those disproportionately bullied are students with disabilities and children who identify with or are perceived as LGBTQ.[63] Bullied children are more likely to suffer from mental health problems, with 41 percent developing social anxiety, 26 percent having suicidal thoughts, and a quarter engaging in self-harm.[64]

☐ *I want to take a stand against bullying and support victims of bullying.*

17. Partnerships for the Goals

a. According to the UN, at the end of 2019, nearly eighty million people worldwide had been forcibly displaced as a result of persecution, conflict, violence, or human rights violations.[65] In fact, the global refugee crisis has now reached a new record high.

> ☐ *I want to help refugees get settled in my community, learn English, find jobs, or receive necessary supplies.*

b. Economies around the world rely on the labor of migrant workers, yet many of these workers end up in legally, economically, and socially vulnerable situations. For instance, 95 percent of the workforce in Qatar is made up of migrant workers, yet the exploitative *kafala* sponsorship system enables widespread abuse and grants excessive power to employers over their employees.[66] Here in the United States, more than half of farmworkers were born outside the country, and 10 percent of the agricultural workforce is here on temporary seasonal labor visas.[67] They are not entitled to overtime pay, rarely receive paid leave if they fall ill, and do not have the federal protection of being able to organize unions.[68]

> ☐ *I want to fight for fair labor laws for farm laborers in the U.S.*
> ☐ *I want labor protection for migrant workers around the world.*

THE ISSUES OR NEEDS THAT MOST RESONATE WITH ME ARE:

_____

_____

_____

—RESOURCES—

If Devon's story struck a chord, get involved with non-profit organizations that fight forced or child marriage, like Unchained at Last (https://www.unchainedatlast.org), or that provide a sanctuary for at-risk youth around the world, like SOS Children's Villages (https://www.sos-usa.org). I sit on the board of SOS U.S. and have seen firsthand what goodness comes from the dedicated people who work on behalf of the kids every day.

If Shannon's pivot towards freeing our oceans from plastics resonated with you, check out SeaChange at https://theseachange.org for more information. You can also get involved with the Ocean Cleanup at https://theoceancleanup.com or volunteer with Ocean Conservancy at https://oceanconservancy.org. Learn more about which plastics are really recyclable at https://apps.npr.org/plastics-recycling/.

To learn more about the organizations with which Harper worked or get involved with the Democratic Republic of Congo, check out congoinitiative.org, easterncongo.org, and healafrica.org.

CHAPTER 3

A Defining Moment

When Offer and Offense fuse, social legacy is born.

*"The place where God calls you is where your deep gladness
and the world's deep hunger meet."*

—FREDERICK BUECHNER

Comfort for the Spirit
Shanghai, China, 2012

The dimpled young man stepped hesitantly into the airy living room and took a deep breath. Even as his palms began to sweat in closed fists held tightly against his sides, he carefully maintained a pleasant smile on his face as he looked around. Just two weeks prior, the young man, Jaesin, had met his housemates through his real estate agent; they were now sharing a bright, comfortable apartment in the convenient Xujiahui district of Shanghai. And after just two weeks of smooth cohabitation, Marie, a slender French girl, had suddenly called the group's first formal meeting. Her thin face was ashen, and her lips were pressed tightly together in distress. Jaesin instinctively knew that something was seriously amiss. Facing her three housemates, all staring expectantly at her, Marie held up her iPad and began to read a news article aloud.

"He has scammed a total of eighty foreign tenants from thirty different Shanghai flats,"[1] she announced in her lightly accented voice. "It appears he has fled Shanghai with over 340,000 yuan [about fifty thousand U.S. dollars] of stolen money. The real landlord of our apartment has already complained to the police. Friends, we are now living here illegally.... We will either have to pay this Ms. Zhang at her standard rental rate, or we will get evicted." The sweaty goateed face of Ryan Fedoruk, the Canadian scam artist, leered at the four young foreigners from Marie's iPad as they realized they had all been defrauded by him.

Seated together in the spacious room, the housemates each absorbed the terrible news in his or her own way. Maxim pushed a pocket of air through his closed lips with an angry pffft. A tall, wiry man, he jumped up from the couch in one swift movement, angrily shouted something in his Eastern European tongue, and stormed out the front door.

Seated beside Jaesin, an Australian woman immediately began scrolling through her cell phone as she muttered furiously under her breath. Looking around, Jaesin sadly thought, "Such dark kibun." The Korean word "kibun" has no direct English translation; it refers to a person's state of mind. In his culture, where harmony is so crucial to interpersonal relationships, an unsettled kibun can disturb the spirit with wounded dignity or the bitterness of disappointment. On one hand, the young Korean man testily reproached himself for having naively sent so much money to a man he had never even met. On the other hand, his thoughts flew despairingly to the future, as he wondered how he could afford to finish his schooling if he were to be evicted. Jaesin's expressive round eyes melted downward at the corners as he slowly sank back into the couch.

The next few days passed in a blur as the housemates met their apartment's real landlord and considered their options for the future. Together, as though they had lived with one another for years, the four foreigners worked to tidy up the space in anticipation of the elderly Ms. Zhang's visit. When their elegantly coiffed landlord met with them, they breathed a collective sigh of relief to find that she was not unreasonable. Though the Shanghainese woman had lost tens of thousands of yuan herself to Fedoruk, she maintained a dignified bearing as she chided the young people for not doing their due diligence. "You cannot trust a laowai [an informal Chinese term for "foreigner"] just because he is a foreigner like yourselves! You should have checked his paperwork and registered with the public security bureau. Then you would have known Fedoruk did not own my apartment." She glared at the young foreigners reproachfully, but then Ms. Zhang's gaze softened as she took in their despondent countenances. "OK, OK," she conceded with a small sigh. "I will give you three days. Then you must pay me or move out."

Maxim and Alice wired money into Shanghai and paid Ms. Zhang, deciding to stay in the apartment that already felt like home. But Marie and Jaesin couldn't afford the same luxury. One night before his eviction, the young Korean man sat at his computer and poured his sorrowful story into an email. His long, slender fingers flew over the keyboard as he connected with all his friends across the vast city of Shanghai. A talented violinist and keyboardist, he had met many people from different walks of life, who had all been brought together through a love of music. And that's how my husband, a bassist who had played in venues there, heard of Jaesin's situation.

— • —

"What do you think? Should we offer him our spare room?" Minki posed the question over dinner. Laini looked up curiously.

"Dad, Rosie just moved out a few months ago. Maybe we should take a break?" Our four-year old's voice lilted sweetly as she proposed the reasonable suggestion. Since we had moved to Shanghai, our spare room had been occupied more often than not.

With concern, I turned to face my daughter. "Do you feel like we need some more family time, Laini?" I was worried that between my busy job at Apple and the other kids we had recently cared for, my own child was feeling neglected.

Our little girl's face broke into a dimpled smile. "Oh no, Mom! Cute baby Rosie *was* part of our family time! I just meant that maybe Dad was tired from all that work taking care of the kids. I think maybe *he* needs a break!"

Minki chuckled and reached over, stroking his thumb over the soft skin of Laini's forearm. "Well, Jaesin is already in his twenties. He's probably pretty self-sufficient!" Then he thoughtfully added, "I think we should do it. Our family always opens our spare room to people who need a safe place to stay."

We all fell silent as his statement sank in. The words rang with a simple truth. Even our four-year-old slowly nodded. Taking a small sip of wine, I thought back to all the occupants of our spare room over the previous thirteen years. Some had been babies, while others had been young adults. Some had borne physical bruises and scars, while others had been weighed down with mental anguish and spiritual trauma. Many had slipped through various cracks of the social justice system. But Minki was right; every one of them had needed a safe place to stay. And that was something our family had been able to offer, time and again.

Seated at our glass dining table that evening, I experienced a defining moment as our family's social legacy sharpened into focus. With sudden clarity, I realized that the people we had met and supported over the years had not been a random series of one-offs. Rather, we had offered something specific to a group of individuals who had needed just that thing. And wherever we had lived, young people in need had found a sanctuary with us.

As a family, we quickly agreed, and Jaesin moved in the next day.

On that winter day as we tried to help him move his things from the elevator lobby into the apartment, Jaesin politely but firmly declined. I sought to break the ice, saying warmly, "Hey, no need to be so formal! We want you to feel comfortable here, so please consider this your home and consider us your friends." In response, the gentle young man looked down, conflicted, then gazed back up at me to state, "But you cannot be my friend."

At first, I was taken aback by his frank statement. But as I listened to Jaesin explain, I received my first lesson in Korean culture. "Age is very important in my culture. In Korea, we can only consider those born in the same birth year as friends. Because you are my elder, I must show you respect as my *nuna*, or elder sister." His voice then took on a tenor of sadness: "Actually, age dictates many expectations in my society. It is one of the challenges with my coming here to learn Chinese this year. In my interest to learn Mandarin, I have created cultural problems back home, and it will be more difficult for me to find a job."

As a Chinese American executive, I found the young man's interest to learn the Chinese language to be mature and forward-looking. After all, how could a deeper understanding of Chinese culture and language *not* be helpful in the future? Just two years prior, China had overtaken Japan to become the world's second-largest economy.

But then I learned from our soft-spoken houseguest that in Korean culture, choosing to take an extra year after college to learn Mandarin was, in fact, seen as countercultural. "Koreans operate within very strict social guidelines," he slowly explained.

Still clustered at the entrance to our apartment, our family stood, listening raptly. Jaesin described how young people back home face stringent time pressure on when they should enter the workforce, get married, and even have a baby. Further, within the Korean business environment, the age hierarchy is even more rigid, with seniority often taking precedence over skill. In a standard Korean company, the youngest employee unquestionably accepts his or her position at the bottom of the totem pole, and everyone naturally assumes his or her place within the chain of command. So, when someone like Jaesin takes extra time off before entering the workforce, he creates an uncomfortable situation by disturbing the clear-cut social framework. After Jaesin completes his Mandarin studies, he will enter the workforce as the newest employee but not the youngest.

I gazed at our new houseguest with renewed respect. "Good for you," I declared with admiration. I wanted to encourage the anxious young man standing before me. "You're doing what you think is right, and I personally believe that learning Mandarin will set you up for *more* opportunities in the future!"

Little Laini chirped from hip height, "Great! Maybe we can come inside the apartment now?" The ice was officially broken as Jaesin's face broke into a huge smile.

Over the next six months, though our houseguest appreciated being able to finish his Chinese education, he sometimes found living with a foreign family to be disconcerting. He watched us closely, the way a curious lab technician might study an unusual science experiment. One day, he unexpectedly returned to the apartment midafternoon and found Minki preparing to pick Laini up from school. "*Hyung*," he hesitatingly addressed Minki with the respectful word for elder brother. "How do you find it, staying at home while your wife goes to work?"

Coming from a heavily patriarchal society, Jaesin observed our family routines with wonder. He saw how Minki walked our daughter to and from school. He contemplated our family structure, in which Dad was the one to organize medical appointments and meet with Laini's teachers after school. And he noticed the way we engaged with our daughter while together.

One day, I overheard Laini chatting with our houseguest. "Why, Jaesin Samchon? Didn't your parents play with you?" she asked "Uncle" Jaesin matter-of-factly as she stacked her blocks into four orderly walls. Sweetly holding her long hair back so it wouldn't obstruct her view, I listened to our houseguest explain: "In Korea, most parents leave their child with grandparents. They come home from work very late at night, so family time together is short. But you are lucky to see both parents every day!"

Pausing to peek at Jaesin through her sleek curtain of hair, Laini replied, "Oh, it's like that for my classmates, too. YuYu's grandma takes care of her, and she only sees her parents on weekends. But I have *three* people at home! Dad and Mom and you." Jaesin had been born with the corners of his lips permanently quirked upward, as though a smile might emerge at any moment. But upon hearing himself included in Laini's family inventory, he grinned delightedly. Then, as his eyes flitted up to notice my profile as I listened from the doorway, he winked at me before turning back to help his little "niece" with her construction.

That evening after Laini went to bed, Jaesin recounted his pre-dinner conversation with our little girl. He said thoughtfully, "You act like a friend to your child. Every moment is like an educational, playful activity. This is very new for me, but I like it very much." Running his elegant fingers through his thick, glossy hair that was not quite a pompadour but puffed upward in hopeful aspiration, he concluded contentedly, "I feel very good *kibun* in your home."

Unfamiliar with the phrase, I refilled his glass from across the table and asked, "What is *kibun*?"

"It is like your mood or state of being," Jaesin explained. He rummaged through his English vocabulary, thoughtfully testing out and discarding words as he slowly continued. "If you hurt someone's *kibun*, you hurt their pride and their spirit will darken. But when you have good *kibun*, you enable others to be in a comfortable state of mind. For instance, in this apartment, I feel good *kibun*.... It is like comfort for the spirit."

There it was, and I loved it! Jaesin had just defined what our spare room was all about. We sought to offer comfort for the spirit to those who needed a safe resting place. I will forever be grateful to my young Korean "brother" for helping us put words to what our family felt called to do. For helping us crystallize our social legacy.

— • —

Jaesin's gentle and thoughtful manner added warmth to our home in countless ways. One spring morning, I found a bowl of perfectly cut watermelon cubes in the refrigerator. I marveled at the flawlessly consistent shapes; whenever I cut watermelon, I invariably end up with a bowl of odd-looking, uneven chunks. And I swear, nicely cut watermelon just tastes better! Then I noticed that each small black seed had been painstakingly removed. Immediately, I knew that this could only be the work of our patient houseguest. And at just four years old, Laini knew it, too.

Skipping into the kitchen, her eyes lit up. "Mom, *xigua shala!* That's for me! Uncle Jaesin makes watermelon salad for me and he takes out all the seeds, so I don't choke on them!" I could only shake my head in astonishment at the exacting work required to assemble the mountain of bright pink, seed-free fruit. As my daughter delicately selected a cube with her forefinger and thumb, she informed me, "His mom used to make watermelon salad for him when he was little, and they call it *soobak hwachae.*" She spoke in that self-assured little-kid voice that rings with confidence when one knows that one is loved. It appeared that comfort for the spirit worked both ways.

With Jaesin in our home, I left for the office with a deeper peace of mind. Minki, rather than finding himself occupied by caring for two little ones, now had help in caring for Laini while I was working. When I had to travel on my frequent business trips, I left the apartment feeling reassured that Laini had two adults at home who loved looking after her.

One Saturday morning, Laini and I were playing school in her room when my iPhone began buzzing insistently. Turning away from the colorful rows of little animals that made up her classroom, I picked up the phone. That morning, our Apple store in Beijing was being overrun with customers, eager to purchase our latest iPhone 4S inventory. And as we had recently called a halt to all iPhone sales in China due to safety concerns, our sensitivity to store disturbances and both customer and employee security was heightened. So, after a few calls with our store's General Manager and public relations team, I decided to jump on a plane that same day to support our store team. Laini's expression turned somber as she listened to my conversations. One small hand reached down and slowly collected slips of homework from her "students," as she clutched a red pen in the other, ready to grade her pupils' papers. For a moment, she looked sadly at a tiny pink bunny named Grace, her favorite student. She loved how I vocalized Grace's squeaky little voice. But then her eyes flitted past my left shoulder and her expression brightened. "Jaesin Samchon, want to play school with me?" she asked.

Thirty minutes later, my daughter hugged me in a brief goodbye and happily went back to teaching her classroom of animals. Jaesin Samchon, his lips upturned in that permanent smile of his, patiently played the role of Teacher's Assistant as he lined up the furry pocket-sized students for recess.

The next evening as I returned home from Beijing, I thought wearily to the week ahead. Monday was full of meetings, and the entire weekend had been eaten up by the challenges in Beijing. Unlocking the door to our apartment, I listened for the sound of little feet running to greet me. But even after I closed the door behind me and hung up my coat, the apartment was unusually quiet.

"Hello? Anyone home?" I called, peering down the hallway. Then I heard Laini's muffled voice come through her closed bedroom door. "Mom, close your eyes and count to ten. Jaesin Samchon and I have a surprise!" Placing my bag on the bench by the door, I obediently closed my eyes and slowly began to count out loud.

"Boo!" they shouted in unison, giggling hysterically as they leaned against each other. I opened my eyes to find Jaesin and Laini standing before me, each wearing a white paper face mask and looking like a gleeful little ghost. That morning, our houseguest had received the wildly popular beauty masks, ordered directly from Korea. He had taught Laini how to unfold the slimy, wet paper, carefully lining up the eyeholes and mouth holes to fit her small face. Together, they had lain on the floor while the masks moisturized their skin. Then, hearing my key in the lock, Jaesin had leaned over, whispering, "Let's go scare your mom! Be very quiet; we will hold hands and then yell 'boo!'" Today, eight years later, every time my daughter sees a face mask, she glances at me with a secret smile and I know exactly whom she's thinking about.

Jaesin not only brought humor and kindness to our home; he also laid down a festive soundtrack to our daily lives. In those months when my Korean little brother lived in our spare room, the apartment was often filled with music. He was an outstanding keyboardist and violinist, and Minki played both guitar and bass. On many evenings, undulating classical melodies or the strum of acoustics greeted me as I stepped out of the elevator after a long day at work. Other times, neighbors stopped by carrying their own gear, and I'd find myself entering a living room crammed with instruments and people, brimming with joyful noise.

On one mid-June evening, I opened the door as I returned home to see Laini pulling out her little violin to participate in the fun. Unable to resist, I stepped out of my heels and quickly assembled my flute to play. "Let's sing my song, Jaesin Samchon!" Laini shouted excitedly. At this, I lowered my flute and tilted my head, watching them and wondering what my daughter's song might be. Then I listened as their voices joined to sing a song I had never heard before. "Mercy is falling like the sweet spring rain!" they sang.

Smiling, I looked to my daughter, her cheeks flushed and eyes sparkling merrily. "Why is that your song?" I asked.

Laini carefully laid her violin and bow on the couch, then bounced over in her flowered sundress to jump in my lap. Weaving her little fingers into my larger ones, she looked up at me, saying, "It's my name! My Korean name is Sweet Rain, right, Jaesin Samchon?"

Minki quickly jumped in: "I asked Jaesin to help us come up with the right Korean name for Laini, since she already has an English and a Chinese name."

Jaesin then explained, "If you're OK with it, I suggested the name Dan-Bi. It means 'sweet rain.'"

A Defining Moment

As Laini sing-songed "Dan-Bi, Dan-Bi" on my lap, I responded, "It's pretty.... I like it. But what's the significance of sweet rain?"

With a bashful smile, Jaesin glanced sideways at me and said, "For the Korean tongue, 'Laini' sounds like 'rainy.'"

I burst out laughing. It was just perfect.

— · —

Dan-Bi, Minki, and I loved sharing our home with Jaesin. He reminded us that giving doesn't always have to feel like a sacrifice. In fact, as givers, we sometimes end up benefiting more than the recipients, when we are living in the center of our personal purpose. Our family has always tried to welcome all the guests in our spare room as though they belonged in our home, but Jaesin truly became a member of the family.

After another month, Shanghai became unendurably hot and sticky as July turned to August. And just when we began to think ahead to fall, Laini's adoptive uncle completed his studies at Donghua University and decided to head back to South Korea.

Though he had received multiple offers to stay and work full-time in China, our friend missed his family and still nursed the boyhood dreams shared by most young men in his home country. Despite his anxieties about joining the workforce later in life, Jaesin still fantasized about securing a job with a big Korean company and getting married to a beautiful Korean woman.

It turned out, his instincts to delay work to learn Mandarin had been spot-on after all. Even as Jaesin's friends cautioned him about the tight job market and his comparably older age, he quickly landed a sales position at one of Korea's biggest chemical companies. In fact, as he moved through the rigorous interview and testing process, Jaesin learned that he was actually allotted extra points for his experience in China.

Two years after he moved out of our apartment, we decided to visit Jaesin in South Korea. Laini missed her uncle, and we were eager to see how he was doing in his new life.

Perhaps time had dulled our memories of the tender but fun-loving man, but his over-the-top greeting at Incheon Airport jolted us right back to those months we had shared in 2012. We stood waiting at the curb, having received a text that he was right around the corner when, with a shout, Jaesin popped his head out of the sunroof of a luxury limousine. His wide-open mouth was stretched in a big, toothy grin. "Hi, hi! Welcome to Korea!" he yelled happily, as other travelers around us leaned in for a closer look.

"Wait!" he then shouted. "Watch this!" His head disappeared back into the limo, and our friend excitedly pushed open the sleek black door. As he did, the song "Gangnam Style" began blasting from the speakers and neon lights swooped maniacally across the interior of the vehicle. Jaesin was truly one of a kind.

Through that trip and over the years, we have shared countless cherished memories with Jaesin. Now the father of two little ones, he continues to enjoy a successful career in South Korea. And I would like to believe that the six kids who have stayed with us since then have benefitted from his influence, too. After all, he helped us define our spare room legacy, and from then on, we sought to provide "comfort for the spirit" to everyone who entered our home.

The Dance
Helmand Province, Afghanistan, 2006

"You hate *all* of them?"

"Yes, every single one! I'd like to kill as many as I could get my hands on."

"Including the women and children?"

"Yes, I'd kill all the women and children."

"Why do you hate Pakistanis so much, Fasil?"

A contemptuous sneer supplanted the Indian man's normally genial smile as he responded, "Pakis are terrorists, every single one of them! They are a failed, miserable country that feeds on violence."

Quentin recoiled in surprise. "Seriously? You can't really believe that. There's not *one* good Pakistani in the whole country?"

"What do *you* think? Indians have become the CEOs of Google, Microsoft, and Pepsi. Pakis are the heads of Taliban, al-Qaeda, and Hizbul Mujahideen," Fasil scornfully replied.

Sensing that the conversation was quickly turning sour, Quentin pivoted to the evening's upcoming event. He was hosting one of his much-anticipated block parties at the old rec center tent that night. Stationed at Camp Leatherneck in Afghanistan, Quentin lived on the base with fifteen thousand other Marines and civilian contractors, where the scorching desert heat, lack of privacy, and constant exposure to danger made everyday life stressful. In part, that's why Quentin's block parties were so well attended. Once a month, he gleefully welcomed Americans, Indians, Russians, and Bosnians into the tent to burn off steam. Just to make it more interesting, the party organizer coordinated a dance throw-down, complete with a cash prize. Tonight, the Marines would be battling it out on the dance floor for a grand prize of five hundred dollars.

Quentin never tired of all the different cultures and languages that coexisted on the base. Sleeping in a one-hundred-man tent, he shared close quarters with people of all nationalities and religious affiliations. Having been raised in Fort Lauderdale, Florida, he found Camp Leatherneck and its potpourri of people a far cry from the poor urban neighbor-hoods of his childhood.

— • —

The youngest of five kids of a single mother, Quentin had moved homes fifteen times with his family before even entering high school. On any given day, the youngster might have attended school in his sister's old shoes, one brother's hand-me-down shirt, and another brother's old jeans. Yet, despite growing up on a tight budget in one of America's most dangerous cities,[2] Quentin never realized how little they had. Surrounded by his siblings and solid in his mother's strict but unwavering love, he learned to navigate the antagonism that existed between his neighborhood and the one that lay east of the turnpike. While there was hostility everywhere in Lauderhill, the Deepside-ver-sus-Shallowside rivalry within the city was profound, and fights often turned deadly.

Though his family couldn't afford the videogames that were so popular back then, Quentin did own a few prized videocas-settes, including the 1984 film *Breakin'*. The young black boy was inspired by the characters of Ozone and Turbo, two street dancers who turn professional. Every day after school, the boy watched street dancers perform in the film; he would pause the tape to mimic the moves when he thought no one was watch-ing. The physical challenge of breakdancing, along with the adrenaline rush that followed his first successful windmills and headspins, provided Quentin with a much-needed escape from the violence that was all around him.

Even as a ten-year-old boy, Quentin could quickly sense the energy building when a fight circle would form in the street. But one day, his mind already on the new dance move he wanted to try when he got home, Quentin stumbled right into a circle.

Heart sinking, he casually sidestepped, trying to ease his way out of the crowd.

But as he listened to the shouting around him, the boy discerned a different kind of excitement. Instead of hearing the enraged clamor of a fight, Quentin stared into enraptured faces of classmates and registered their exultant whoops with confusion. Peering into the middle of the circle, he observed two guys moving with a full-body fluidity, instead of the choppy punches and kicks he was expecting. And just as the sixth grader realized he had chanced upon a dance circle, someone shoved him hard from behind.

Suddenly finding himself the center of attention, Quentin spontaneously pulled a few moves he'd been practicing at home. Eyes widened and the kids from school hollered with appreciation, witnessing his dance moves for the first time. And just like that, Quentin discovered both his tribe of friends and the hobby that would eventually save his life.

As the street violence escalated in middle school, he found refuge in dance. It kept him off the streets and gave him an anchor to avoid the drugs that ensnared so many of his schoolmates. But the pressure cooker that was his community constantly threatened to boil over. It felt as if the world were on fire.

One Monday afternoon when he was sixteen and a high school senior, eyeing a water fountain through a Marine recruiting station's front window, Quentin wandered in. Knowing nothing about the military, he took in the photos around him and glimpsed a dramatically different future. Having no plans after high school graduation, he listened intently as a sergeant laid out all the benefits afforded by the Marine Corps. After he paused for a reaction, the teen asked just one question, "How quickly can I ship out?"

Four short days later, Quentin was on a plane. Not knowing where he was going, and with no long-term plan, he moved with confidence, knowing that wherever he would end up was likely to be better than where he had been. In fact, he hadn't even heard about the notorious Marine Corps boot camp when he had signed up. Yet, the boy from Deepside advanced with ease through twelve weeks of grueling drills and tests. Having grown up amidst the dangers of his old neighborhood and answering to the best drill instructor on the planet, his mother, boot camp felt like child's play.

Quentin began his military career in logistics, where he learned to fix anything that needed repairing, from broken weapons to camp generators. Soon, his skills and likeable nature opened the door to Marine Security Guard duty, and he joined the Marine Corps Special Operations Command (MARSOC). At the age of nineteen, Quentin became an Operator who worked missions, and it was there he would serve for the next eight years.

In fact, it was in MARSOC where Quentin first met Fasil. A short Indian engineer with a little square head, Fasil appeared to try to make up for his lack of stature with heavily gelled hair that was comically slicked straight up. Drawn to the endearing Indian man, Quentin held out his hand in introduction. He instantly knew they'd create a fun work environment together when Fasil shook his hand, saying, "I know MLK; I'm a brother, too!" Laboring for hours in the field together, the unlikely friends developed the foundations of a lasting relationship.

On the morning of the dance-off, Fasil coyly strutted into work, walking in an oily way that seemed to lead from the hip. Looking up and smiling, Quentin paused in his work to ask, "What are *you* so proud of today?"

Jutting out his posterior and striking a dramatic pose, the small Indian man pointed proudly to his acid-washed jeans. "Just got a care package from home. Check out my new jeans."

Now openly chuckling, Quentin replied, "Man, those are *women's* jeans! I can see everything from your *front* pockets in your *back* pockets!"

Completely unfazed, Fasil replied, "Well, they look *good*. I'm wearing them tonight, and they're going to help me win the cash prize."

In the earlier days of the block parties, those in the tent seemed to section themselves off with invisible partitions. The Eastern Europeans gathered in one corner, while Americans chugged beers in another. Indians danced together, arms slung casually over one another's shoulders, while Pakistanis stood on the other side of the tent, watching warily. But after a few months, when Quentin and his friend Daryl concocted the idea of a dance-off, those invisible dividers slowly began to dissolve.

A circle inevitably formed as the more confident dancers claimed their stage in the middle of the floor. Shouts of encouragement rang out as Bosnian men threw down with German women. Brazilian breakdancers exchanged moves with Japanese street dancers. And sometimes as folks headed back to the sleep tents late at night, Quentin and Daryl smiled, watching new friends stumbling out of the tent together in happy exhaustion.

Quentin could see how good the block parties were for the camp, and he knew he was contributing in a way that brought the best of his unique talents to the community. But one night above all others served as a defining moment for him.

The party was in full swing and people everywhere were rocking, spinning, and jiving as they warmed up for the dance-off. Suddenly, it felt as though the evening stopped in a freeze frame. The lights seemed to dim, and Quentin's peripheral vision slowed as he eyes locked on a pair of bodies gyrating on the other side of the room. Rocking out to "Black and Yellow," Fasil, in his acid-washed women's jeans, was dancing joyfully with a Pakistani.

Seventy years of fastidiously cultivated hatred, battle-weary national borders, and uncompromising cultural barriers all came tumbling down. The impossible had happened, fueled by the universal language of movement. In that moment, surrounded by hot, sweaty bodies and energized by the thumping music, Quentin felt his purpose click. He would bring his love of dance to help bridge societal, cultural, and economic differences.

— . —

The Marine carefully bided his time. After eight years and having worked in Afghanistan for so long that he became a permanent resident, Quentin exited the military and returned to America. Soon after resettling into civilian life, the dancer seized an opportunity to join a nonprofit organization on a visit to Uganda. Arriving at the country's largest refugee settlement, Nakivale, he quickly organized movement workshops, demonstrating how dance can be used to express pain, encourage compassion, and support a community in healing. Soon after, floating on the success of his Ugandan workshops, Quentin visited Congo, Somalia, and Burundi.

As the African workshops gained momentum, Quentin continued to refine his Offer. He evolved his live teaching sessions with the aid of virtual reality, to orchestrate cross-cultural exposure. Soon, he was able to bring refugee Africa to Caucasian kids in Middle America, enabling dialogue and understanding through shared experiences. The children's camaraderie reminded Quentin of the kinship developed in his block party dance-offs back in Afghanistan. And he wanted more.

A Defining Moment

"How can I bottle this and do it for the rest of my life?" he wondered. "These kids will become America's future business leaders. They'll be our policemen and -women, our policymakers and judges. If we can build that cultural sensitivity and appreciation now, my movement will foster something that's truly lasting."

And so, Quentin established a nonprofit organization, Movements 4 Movements (M4M). Right away, he was invited to facilitate retreats and workshops all over North and South America. At workshops in public high schools he conducted more recently, he witnessed new levels of understanding unfolding between teachers and students who saw each other every day yet struggled to understand one another. As he watched, Quentin marveled, "Cultural barriers aren't just impediments that need to be broken down between Indians and Pakistanis from two war-torn countries. Movement can help us find unity through compassion, right here in our daily lives."

As teachers and students embraced a new mode of communication through movement, one teacher realized that a problem student of hers was, in fact, homeless. She was chagrined to discover that he wasn't derelict in his studies; rather, he just didn't have a place to do his homework in the evenings. Another student finally revealed to his teacher that he didn't have enough to eat at home. So, when his snacks were confiscated in class, what was perceived as a disrespectful response was, in fact, panic. His only sustenance for the day had been torn from his hands. And every time Quentin witnessed reconciliation through new understanding, he felt affirmed in the social legacy he sought to create with his life's work.

Since that defining moment in a hot, sweaty tent in Afghanistan, Quentin has been living out his personal purpose every day. He's building his social legacy in M4M, through which he uses dance and movement to overcome misunderstandings, cultural barriers, and socioeconomic differences.

A Voice for the Voiceless
Montreal, Canada, 2013

Hot tears rushed to the surface of her dark, smoky eyes as the company of acrobats, dancers, techies, and musicians gave her one final standing ovation. The slender artist bowed her head, humbly accepting her peers' recognition. And as her friends whooped and clapped, she allowed herself to breathe in these final, precious moments.

With one last smile, Tara blew a kiss, turned, and quietly walked offstage. As the first Indian music artist to have joined Cirque du Soleil, she felt her heart swell with pride when she thought about the company's *Koozå* production. She not only had contributed to inventing a new language and a unique transcultural sound for the show, but had brought her vision to life as a lead singer for the production. And in doing so, she had crafted an international spotlight for future Asian performing artists. Yet now, as Tara stepped off set and headed home, her mind pivoted to a young woman known as Nirbhaya. The musician thought back to her defining moment just a few weeks prior. She had resolved to pivot the direction of her life as her Offer and Offense had merged. The artist would draw from her decades of experience as a storyteller in the entertainment space to tell Nirbhaya's tale, and to speak out against the urgent reality of violence against women.

— • —

Tara's musical career began when she was just fourteen years old. The serious young girl had studied theater, music, and elocution for as long as she could remember, passionately absorbing the many languages and musical influences of India. From the spirited folk music of the mountains to serious Indian classical constructs, an intoxicating swirl of sound illuminated the girl's childhood. She learned to love jazz, even as her first piano teacher introduced her to the restless drama of Mozart and dreamy landscapes of Satie. But it was the girl's guitar teacher who first brought Tara to a recording studio.

Within a year, she had signed on to represent iconic brands like Pepsi and L'Oréal with her distinctive, sotto voice. Advertising jingles and voiceovers provided a steady source of income for Tara into her college years. In addition, the commercial work provided her with invaluable lessons on how to engage listeners across the many strata of society, and how to create memorable and resonant one-line captions. And though, at times, Tara's pursuit of individual expression differed from her clients' needs, those creative collaborations also fortified her ability to create music that was appealing to the masses. In the future, the young performer would discover that this unique combination of training would serve her very well.

Soon after she graduated college, Tara signed on as a lead singer-songwriter with Mrigya, an Indian global music band. With her love of diverse musical genres, she found joy in creating unique soundscapes by blending elements of Indian, Celtic, jazz, and rock traditions. With them, at the age of twenty-one, she flew to England on her first international music tour, where the band was recognized with a number of prestigious awards. But after a few years, despite media accolades and broad global recognition, Tara once again began to feel confined.

As a child musician, her independent style had developed even as it sought to emerge from within commercial music classifications, the way a butterfly strengthens its wings by beating against its cocoon. Now, as she sought to broaden her individual style and leverage the Mrigya platform to talk about the things that really mattered to her, the sensuously beautiful singer felt categorized and limited within the industry's musical genres. Tara had been born with an exceptional musical gift, which had only been amplified through her advertising and indie band experiences. Yet she strained to find her place in the world, where her Offer might meet a truly worthy need.

Then, Cirque du Soleil called. The French-accented male voice of composer Jean-François Côté explained, "We're designing our twentieth production, which explores themes of unity, identity, collaboration, and empowerment." Tara immediately perked up at the substantive themes and listened intently.

The expressive voice in her ear continued, "I want to create something utterly original; I will bring international artists together to blend electronic music with Western pop, orchestral symphonies, and Indian classical, folk, and contemporary traditions." Côté then asked, "So, would you be interested in joining the *Koozå* team?"

As she digested the man's remarkable vision, Tara's heart skipped a beat. This could be the opportunity she'd been yearning for, a chance to fuse different genres and breathe her own brand of creativity into a newly formed production. J. F. was more than persuasive and understood Tara's need for creative integrity. The offer to engage with the incredible lineup he had put together, combined with the opportunity to represent her South Asian heritage and culture on an international platform, proved irresistible.

As they began working together, the Cirque du Soleil composer drew out Tara's unique mixture of layered originality and appreciated her aptitude for creating simple hook lines that people of all languages could sing. In the early days of creation, Côté watched the woman whose pencil raced furiously across the page, as thick, cascading waves of hair shrouded her face. And when Tara integrated all her musical and theatrical influences, he not only accepted her creativity but eagerly pushed the limits of her imagination for more.

As Tara worked with the band on developing the musical score each day, she often visited the other performers as they practiced their unique acts. With her eyes trained on the tightrope walkers who rehearsed thirty feet in the air above her, the musician's lips moved steadily as they shaped new words for Cirque's tradition of invented languages. Fashioning new tongues by drawing upon Hindi, Urdu, English, French, Spanish, and Portuguese phonetics, Tara's bowed lips pulled apart and reconstructed sounds the way an engineer might delicately disassemble and then restore a complex piece of machinery.

As she tapped the connective bridges of her Indian heritage for *Koozå*, it was clear to the entire cast that in her quiet, deliberate way, Tara handled this responsibility with utmost care and respect. She treasured the latitude she had been given to create something entirely unique, a new language and fresh formats that would enable meaningful cultural dialogue.

After months of development, Cirque introduced *Koozå* to the world, and it quickly became a successful, popular show. Along with the striped Innocent character and infamous Wheel of Death, Tara's otherworldly voice soon became recognizable to thousands. Sometimes her sweet, ethereal notes lilted tenderly toward the domed ceiling. Other times her soulful voice projected poignantly across the theater, rich and velvety in its texture. Together with the rest of the cast, she performed for more than two thousand people twice a day across three continents.

Tara found this new creative outlet fulfilling, and soon she also discovered a deeper purpose in her job. Spending so much time with her fellow performers, the singer forged a connection with the younger women of the cast. Intimately familiar with the stresses and vulnerabilities faced by young performing artists, especially while traveling alone on tour, Tara sought to create a safe, nurturing space for the women who confided in her. And with each new city, she designed nature and art walks for them, supplemented by group physical health sessions. Tara had naturally donned the role of older sister within her creative community.

— · —

Then, everything changed on December 16, 2012. That day, Tara was seated in London's iconic Royal Albert Hall, taking a short break between rehearsals. Sliding down on the red velvet seat, the willowy singer rested the back of her head on the soft cushion. She gazed admiringly up at the expansive fluted roof of the historic building. That evening, the cast would be performing in this majestic space, where the world's greatest artists have made history, from Rachmaninoff in the early 1900s to Eric Clapton and David Bowie in more recent years. Suddenly, she became aware of an insistent buzzing. The indigo screen of her mobile phone lit up with alerts.

Something the media was referring to as "the Nirbhaya rape" had begun to rage across India like a firestorm. Frowning, Tara tapped a link and began to read. In the next few minutes, as she digested the story of a twenty-three-year-old physiotherapy intern's gang rape, Tara felt her stomach muscles tighten in horror. The sheer brutality of the attack had shocked the nation. Six men not only had gang-raped a young woman but had tortured her, using an iron rod to tear apart her insides. Much later, when the young woman was found on the side of the road half dead, her shredded intestines lay on the road beside her body.

When Tara's eyes landed on a photo of where the girl had been found, her body went cold and deathly still all at once. Those abominable acts of violence had all happened just two blocks from her parents' home in India.

A Defining Moment

Over the next few days, even as she threw herself into two performances a day in the great hall, Tara followed the news as Delhi came to a standstill. The savage nature of the Nirbhaya crime had galvanized unprecedented national outrage and an outpouring of protests over the longstanding issues of sexual violence and treatment of women in India. And since Indian law did not allow the press to publish the victim's name, the young intern had become publicly known as Nirbhaya ("fearless").

By the end of the week, the endless stream of news from back home had awakened long-forgotten memories from Tara's own childhood. Once again, her heart pumped furiously in her throat as she remembered walking in the capital's streets at night, quickening her pace as shadows shifted menacingly around her.

Late that evening, an unrelenting question pierced Tara's heart as she soaked in a hot bath: "The things I'm choosing to sing about, the platform to which I have access...how can I use it to shift the needle? How can I use my skills to help?" That week had become a defining moment for the artist. For over two decades, she had honed all that she had to offer creatively and musically as a designer and performer in the entertainment space. Now, she deeply felt the need to create for purpose. And as thousands of Indians flooded the streets, demonstrating in her hometown, Tara saw the opportunity to use her talents to facilitate betterment for women. She thought back to her teenage years, when even then she had sought to use music, and the stage, to express discontent with all she perceived was wrong in her society. She reflected on the years when she had felt typecast and somehow restrained from singing about the things that mattered most to her. Now, as a mature and accomplished professional, coming off six years of performing with Cirque du Soleil, Tara felt her creative Offer and Offense fuse as her social legacy emerged, unveiling a new vision for her next chapter.

So, the beloved singer and musician, who had nurtured so many of the young women's voices in the troupe, resigned from Cirque. For the first time in her life, completely uninhibited in expression and delivering against no one else's brief, Tara threw back her head and laughed as she felt her spirit soar. "I will lend my voice to the voiceless," she declared to the empty room. Quivering in unchecked awakening, her slender fingers found her computer's keyboard, and Tara began to type: "In and through artistry, I will create for impact."

Rémi, her life partner, whom she had met at Cirque and with whom she had toured all these years, now sat beside her, and together they began to dream. Sharing the same passion for using creativity purposefully, the couple sketched the outline for what would become an agency called LembasWorks.

And long into the evening, the artists worked, thoughtfully detailing their goals. Alongside Tara's artistic vision, Tara and Rémi also defined their business ambitions. While providing novel platforms for women in their industry, this new company would redefine success, prioritizing goodness and sustainability alongside profit. It would establish new standards in industry production, protecting the environment as they connected the worlds of entertainment and business. But first... first, Tara would compose the song for Nirbhaya that had been restlessly stirring in her soul for weeks.

That night, in a mere ten minutes, the song "My Kind" was written. Much as the rape case had shattered a dam of suppressed expression in India, Tara felt her own emotions crest as she gave voice to a declaration of empowerment that was both intimately personal and abundantly universal.

Two years later, she released her *Quest: Origins* album featuring the song. In that same year, due to its eco-responsible, interactive design, Lembas was invited to present in Paris as a "Creator as Catalyst for Change." Tara's social legacy was flourishing.

Since then, between large-scale corporate and civil programs, Tara has followed her heart on special projects, continuing to give a voice to the voiceless. In 2016, she traveled to New Delhi, India, where the singer performed her music for vulnerable abandoned and orphaned girls. The musician was deeply touched when she heard how female business executives stepped up to keep the children out of orphanages, each choosing to mother over a dozen girls in a home environment. Bringing in the Lembas team and collaborators to volunteer from around the globe, she created music and design workshops for the girls, encouraging them to envision their future as female leaders in creativity and technology.

Then, in 2017, Tara returned to the girls, now one year older. After listening to their life updates, she spent an afternoon singing the songs they loved. One by one, the young women joined Tara's softly haunting voice, as together they sang the lyrics of "My Kind":

> This time is my time, this space is my space
> This feud is my feud, make no mistake
> Given to this truth and a will that won't be tamed
> A voice meant to be heard, a voice that won't be shamed
> Proud, she runs free...unfettered, unframed.

—REFLECTION—

As you made your way through this chapter, did a defining moment in your life come to mind? Was there a moment when you realized your Offer and your Offense came together in a meaningful purpose? As the opportunity presented itself, did you embrace it or perhaps, distracted by the busyness of life, push it to the back of your mind?

Or possibly, you have yet to experience a defining moment. Maybe you're having that moment right now. Let's consolidate the work you did in Chapters One and Two to see what emerges.

Please fill in the left side of the graphic below with your output from Chapter One, and the right side with your output from Chapter Two. Then take a stab at writing down what you think your social legacy might be.

> **What if you were a stone in the lake?**
>
> *Have you ever tossed a stone into a lake, listening for that satisfying plop as it's eagerly gulped by the body of water? Do you remember the ripples that your stone created, undulating outward? What if your social legacy were that stone? Can you envision the ripple effect of your conviction?*

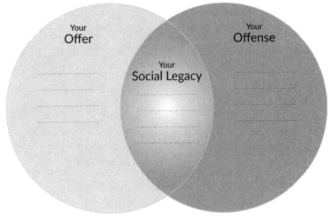

Figure 3.1

A Defining Moment

As an example, here is how I define my social legacy, with the help of my family, Lia, Devon, and Jaesin.

Figure 3.2

If you have identified your social legacy, try slotting it into this sentence:

I will extend _____ [my Offer] to address the issue of _____ [my Offense] in order to _____ [effect the impact I want to have].

What if failure were your best guidepost?

It's human nature to avoid dwelling on our failures, and as we look back in time, we sometimes gloss over those moments to avoid becoming ensnared in negative emotion. But what if those milestones in our life actually served to direct us toward our social legacy? What if, instead of circumventing those moments, we stopped to examine them? We could identify areas where we don't thrive and contexts that don't play to our strengths.

As you deliberate over these exercises, here are a few thought starters:

- What if you were suddenly placed in front of thirty students and instructed to teach a one-hour class on a subject of your choosing? What are your teachable ideas?
- What if your life were a movie? What would be its title?
- What if the movie of your life were played in reverse? How would it end?

> **What if there were no compromises?**
>
> *Some of us live for today, serving our own happiness. Others prioritize self-sacrifice, maintaining an austere lifestyle.*
>
> *But what if living out your social legacy both served others and enriched your life with joy and meaning?*
>
> *(Spoiler alert: I think it does.)*

- And what if you could view your entire movie frame by frame? Which segments would you want to cut out or fast-forward through? On the other hand, which good or worthy moments would you wish to extend or feature in the trailer?
- When are you at your very best? What are the conditions that set you up for those moments?
- Who in your life is proud of you, and why?
- Who is your hero, and why? What aspects of this person would you most like to reflect?
- Whose approval do you most seek, and what would that person say about you today?
- What would his or her reaction to your social legacy be?

—RESOURCES—

Did Jaesin's story pique your interest in hosting an international student? You can learn more about the Host Family Program provided by Education First at https://www.ef.edu/host-family/hosting-international-students/. For other options, check out https://www.afsusa.org/about-afs/ or https://iseusa.org/about-ise/.

Were you inspired by Quentin's social legacy? Learn more or get involved at https://www.movements4movements.com.

If you'd like to learn more about Tara's work, check out her website at https://www.lembas.ca.

CHAPTER 4

The First Step

Take the first step toward your social legacy.

"From a little spark may burst a mighty flame."

—DANTE ALIGHIERI

A Place to Die
Shanghai, China, 2012

"Mom, who is that baby you talking about?" Laini's little voice chirped as she entered the room.

My husband and I exchanged uneasy glances. Seated in the kitchen, we hadn't realized our three-year-old had overheard the phone conversation. That morning for the first time in years, we had declined to help care for a vulnerable child.

We had just heard about the eighteen-month-old boy, Teo, who had been born with a debilitating disability. He was completely immobile and in constant agony from an operation gone wrong. Chances were, he wasn't going to make it and simply needed a safe place to pass. I shared the highlights with Laini, closing with, "Babe, I think it may just be too much for us."

My toddler looked at me with disbelief and said, "Mom, he's all alone and *hurting*. What if that was *me!?* Would you leave *me* there?" I had never seen my daughter look so incensed. So, when she declared, "Let's go get him. *Right now!*" that's exactly what we did.

— · —

As we settled Teo into the apartment, a healthcare worker educated us on his condition. The infant had been born with extreme hydrocephalus, which literally means "water in the head"—"hydro" meaning water and "cephalus" referring to the head. With this condition, the head swells up when excess cerebrospinal fluid builds up in the cavities of the brain.

We learned that hydrocephalus isn't a terribly unusual diagnosis. In fact, the National Institute of Neurological Disorders and Stroke estimates that one in every five hundred children is affected.[1] But most cases are diagnosed early, some even before birth, and they can be managed quite effectively. The problem area can be treated either by removing the cause of fluid obstruction or by installing a shunt to divert the fluid away from the brain.

Nearly two years prior, Teo's parents, unlike many in China who rationalized discarding a handicapped baby to try again for a healthy son, had done the best they could. After saving up their money over an arduous sixteen months, they handed their baby boy to a doctor who promised to install a shunt in the boy's skull. The shunt would slowly drain the cerebrospinal fluid from his head into his stomach, from where it would pass harmlessly through his body. And though his surgery was happening much later than was ideal, his skull would hopefully shrink to a more normal size.

For many in the Western world, the idea of discarding a baby seems barbaric and unthinkable. But Teo had been born during the period in which the Chinese government had imposed a one-child policy. Further, since China does not offer a social security system, a child becomes his or her aging parents' only source of support and security in their later years. So, with all three individuals' futures riding on the health and future earning potential of that one child, parents felt immense pressure to ensure that their one baby was as strong and healthy as possible, and sometimes abandoned or killed their handicapped or female babies to try again.

When his parents picked Teo up after his surgery, the anxious couple was aghast to find a hole drilled through their baby's skull. But the doctor reassured them that the shunt was installed where it should be and so, with fear plaguing their thoughts and hope swelling in their hearts, they brought him home.

But after just a few days, it was clear that Teo was not thriving. His head was as enlarged as before the surgery; it was so swollen that his eyes still couldn't close...not to blink, and not even to sleep. But whereas before he would lie silent, occasionally following them with his eyes, the baby now screamed in pain. He refused to drink anything and was becoming dangerously dehydrated. Finally his parents, left with an empty bank account and dashed expectations, bleakly dropped Teo off at a nearby orphanage.

The receiving caregivers took one look at Teo and knew instantly that a shunt had not been installed. Then, seeing the hole that had been callously drilled into the baby's head, they placed him to the side and focused on the hundreds of healthier orphans.

This decision wasn't made out of heartlessness, but with so many requiring attention and not enough caregivers, those in charge had learned to assess each baby and assign their desperately limited resources the best they could.

Luckily for Teo, China also benefits from some incredible nonprofit organizations that care specifically for marginalized children. A member of one such organization was doing the rounds and came across Teo lying in a corner. Distressed at the dire situation, this organization immediately began outreach, and we were one of the families called.

The team of passionate caregivers was simply fabulous. When they dropped him off at our apartment, reconstructive surgery had already been scheduled and paid for, despite concerns that the baby was already beyond the point of possible recovery. They also provided medicine for his seizures, infant formula, and diapers. Literally all we had to do was love and care for the baby.

So that's what we did. My husband spent countless hours lying on the floor next to Teo, holding up an iPad to engage and stimulate him. My daughter invested more hours than I thought possible for such a little girl, patiently playing with him and "reading" him books.

But the little guy came with his unique set of challenges. When Teo first came to us, he hated eating or drinking, often crying hysterically as soon as he caught sight of a bottle. We soon realized that Teo had only ever eaten in a supine position. So, as an experiment to understand what he was experiencing, our family took turns trying to eat while lying flat on our backs. We each gasped and choked painfully when it came to our turn. No wonder the little guy was malnourished; we discovered that it is virtually impossible to eat or drink while lying down! That same day, we went out and bought him a reclining high chair. And while, in those early days, it was sometimes difficult to gauge what Teo understood, it seemed clear that he delighted in joining us at the dinner table! His floppy little feet kicked, and he gurgled his signature "ha huh...ha huh" while large, unblinking eyes rotated to take everything in.

Soon, Teo discovered a newfound love of food. It seemed like he was making up for lost time. We taught him the American

Sign Language sign for "more," and he signed it. All. The. Time. And he *meant* it—he wanted more. Of everything. Then Laini took it upon herself to teach Teo how to hold a bottle. One day, she solemnly informed me, "Mom, I could do it when I was little. He has some special needs, but his arms work just fine." Every single day, I could hear her saying to him, "Teo, *zi ji na*" ("hold it yourself").

And I'll never forget the day he first did. I was in the kitchen on a Saturday morning, preparing breakfast while distractedly scrolling through emails with one hand. Standing next to Teo's high chair in the next room, Laini suddenly squealed in delight: "He's doing it, Mom! He's doing it! *Ta zi ji na le!*"

I peered around the corner, and my face split into a huge grin, watching her do a funny little victory dance as her brother precariously balanced a bottle in his tiny hands. Even more hilarious, he was doing his funny little chortle, "ha huh, ha huh," as the formula dribbled in white rivulets down his chin.

Sometimes in life, you get the big victories. And at other times, you revel in the little ones. Oh, how indescribably sweet those moments can be. The baby who came to our home to die was now holding his own bottle and feeding himself!

That wasn't the only time Laini's faith and perseverance paid off. Every Saturday morning, she found him lying on our thick striped rug in the family room. She'd position herself on her back, then pin her small arms under her. I'd watch as she'd turn her head to look at Teo and say, "Watch, Teo. Watch *jie-jie*." He'd watch his *jie-jie*, his elder sister, as she rocked back and forth, until she gained enough momentum to roll over her shoulder...right onto her face.

I savored his little "ha huh, ha huh" and noticed with interest that he was really paying attention. He watched as she rolled onto her stomach and then slowly turned her head to face him, resting her cheek on the carpet. From the doorway, I smiled at the lilt in her muffled voice: "See, Teo? See how you roll over?"

Once again, Laini's tenacity paid off. Despite the incredible weight of his liquid-filled head, Teo learned to roll over. For some reason, though, he could roll in only one direction. So, he'd roll and roll until he hit a barrier: a piece of furniture, a wall, or an ornery dog. Then he'd grunt and chortle patiently until one of us noticed and helped him turn around.

At that point, I was working as the Chief Commercial Officer for InterContinental Hotels Group (IHG) in Greater China. Looking after a portfolio of six hotels, four loyalty programs, and an extended sales and marketing team of over five thousand employees, I often took calls on my way home and sifted through a mental catalog of business challenges and meeting follow-ups from the day. But as soon as the door closed behind me, those issues settled in the back of my mind to rest for a while, as my little guy rolled toward me and Laini danced over to show me her latest jewelry creation.

As a working mother, I visualize my life as a beach. Working in the soft, silky (and sometimes hot!) sand all day, I return home in the evenings to swim in the warm waters of my family. So, as I step into our home, the waves of my family wash over me. Water and sand converge, sparkling in beautiful streaming lines. Adding Teo to the family just made the whole thing so much more magical.

— • —

Those early days were just miraculous. We watched as our amazing little boy learned to manipulate those wriggling, waving things in front of his eyes…. Soon, he began to control movement in his fingers and arms. We watched Laini help turn Teo's body around when he'd rolled up against the wall.

And we watched his adoring eyes follow the unceasing movements of her small, energetic body every minute she was in the room.

But not all our days were sweet discovery and development. Teo did have a proper shunt installed after he moved in, but the pressure in his head was still immense. The shunt also needed to be adjusted, so sometimes it allowed the liquid to move a little too quickly, or a little too slowly. All of this put him in dreadful pain and distress.

For months, he'd scream every hour, nearly on the hour like a nightmarish cuckoo clock.

Midnight.

One a.m.

Two a.m.

We'd jolt awake, hearing him scream "*Nooooo!*" Then either Minki or I would rush to scoop him up—the small ten-pound body and the big ten-pound head. We'd try to comfort our tiny boy, who stared bug-eyed up at us in the dark, moonlit room. I'll confess, that distorted face, though heartbreakingly sweet and precious, could at times also be jarring as his huge, unblinking eyes glowed luminously in the dark room.

Eventually, the surge of pain would come to an end and Teo would settle down. But because his head was still so distended that his eyes couldn't close, it was impossible to tell if he had finally fallen back to sleep. Sometimes, after twenty minutes of softly crooning to him, I'd slowly lay him back in his crib and leave him to sleep with his eyes staring, wide open. Other times I'd place him back in the crib and he'd start shrieking immediately, never having been lulled back to sleep.

Our entire family suffered pretty exhausting sleep deprivation for a few months, but not one of us complained…. After all, we could see the toll Teo's pain was taking on him. A little tiredness was no comparison. None at all.

During this time, I also realized that where we work and for whom we work make all the difference. My boss, Kenneth, the CEO of IHG Greater China, was a man of compassion and understanding. He had met my family and was so gracious to me when I came in looking a little haggard. He often asked after my family, and made a point to visit my office when Teo was in the building. Because of Kenneth, I was able to integrate work and life, creating a lifestyle and charting a calendar that worked both for the business and for my family. He allowed me to bring my full self to work, and in the process, serve as a role model to our teams for how head and heart can come together in leadership. I am still so grateful to him for expanding the boundaries of a professional work relationship to allow for personal engagement and care.

And that time paid off, because despite his physical discomfort and challenges, our little boy continued to flourish. Months prior, we had taken that first step in bringing him home, not knowing where the journey was headed and not expecting it to last more than a few days. But then we grew with him as he graduated from rolling to pushing himself up on his belly. Imagine tummy time with a ten-pound dumbbell affixed to your head. He'd grit his teeth and push himself up, arms shaking. And after a while, the strength in his arms and core, combined with a shunt that was effectively draining the fluid from his head, enabled our boy to develop the "army tadpole" move.

Teo discovered this special way of moving across the floor. He'd push up on his hands, put one arm in front, collapse on his forearm, and then throw his other forearm forward. Next, as he pulled with all his upper-body might, he'd wiggle his lower half forward.

As Teo discovered mobility, his personality began to shine. He started uttering a few simple words: "Dada," "Mama," and "*jie-jie*"; he had learned to summon and engage his family! And boy, did he revel in it. He'd often call one of us just to crack up in delight when we came running. For the first time, Teo had claimed a degree of control in his life.

And it only got better. He started sitting all the way up, just about at the same time he outgrew the largest stroller we had been able to find for him. And so, we prepared to transition our son to his first wheelchair. We swapped the extra-extra-large stroller for an extra-extra-small wheelchair. And I'll never forget the day we brought that red plaid wheelchair home.

Laini, who had recently lost her babyish lisp, grasped my hand and protested, "Mom, I don't *want* him in a wheelchair!" When I asked her why, my daughter sadly responded, "I won't be able to stand on the footrest anymore and play with him while you push us."

I thought about how sweet the pair of them were, Laini always standing on the stroller's footrest, leaning down towards Teo to talk with him, her long hair tickling his face as we crossed the hectic streets of Shanghai. I told Laini, "That's OK, love. You'll have lots of other times in the day to play with him. And maybe you can help me push the wheelchair! That's a really important job."

I was mentally congratulating myself on the smooth parenting pivot when she suddenly burst into tears. "Mom, why don't you *understand*?! I don't stand on the stroller to *play* with him.... I'm blocking him from all the mean people who stare at him and call him *names*! How am I gonna *protect* him if he's in a wheelchair? They'll all be able to *see* him sitting *right there!*" Laini sobbed, and her hands clenched into fists as though her heart had broken with the very thought.

Which broke *my* heart. My five-year-old's tender sensitivity took my breath away. All those walks, when I thought she just wanted to play with him as I pushed the stroller, she had been *shielding* him.

Once we wiped away our tears, Laini and I had one of our best conversations ever. We talked about how we can't always stand in front of the ones we love, blocking them from the world and protecting them. Sometimes, we need to stand alongside them as they face personal challenges head-on. We talked about how we can also stand behind them, letting them know we have their backs and reassuringly offering our support and unconditional love.

I watched the comprehension light up her eyes. Laini nodded resolutely and said, "OK, Mom. I'll push Teo's wheelchair and *always* have his back; *that* will be my job from now on."

I think it was approximately four days later when I was finally able to collect my melted heart off the floor and shove it back into my chest cavity.

— • —

As Teo learned to sit up with a degree of stability, he also graduated from his high chair to one of three small red plastic chairs that came with a tiny green table our dear friend had gifted to Laini when she was little.

And we sure weren't about to leave Teo sitting by himself! So, our entire family shared meals at this tiny green table. Now, I'm not a big person by any definition, but I felt huge, with my knees scrunched up against my chest, eating off bright IKEA plasticware. During the day, I walked to meetings in my four-inch stilettos and sat on Herman Miller chairs. In the evening, I practically squatted in a tiny plastic chair, barefoot and giggling with the kids. But it was perfect: Teo was in his element at the table. He was now able to sit up and feed himself, even swapping his bottle for a sippy cup! The kid was moving up in the world, fast.

Each time Teo uttered a new word at dinner, we'd write it down on the whiteboard over his seat. It started with just three words, then ten words.... Eventually the list grew to forty-five, to ninety-eight, to a whopping 196 words! After dinner, Laini was allowed the responsibility of preparing Teo's antiseizure medicine. He didn't seem to mind the flavor of his "meh-meh," and watched his *jie-jie* with huge, expectant eyes as she carefully measured out his dose and fed it to him each night. Teo was now sitting upright for most of the day and sleeping peacefully through each night. As we witnessed his continued improvement, we decided it was time to get him a therapy bike. This pedal-less, three-wheeled device with extra sturdy handles allowed Teo to get around in a completely new way. And life in our small apartment changed immediately.

— • —

The excited boy was suddenly everywhere. He did need help mounting the bike, but once on, Teo was a beast. He'd bike into the kitchen and ask for "sah" (snacks). He'd follow his sister around until she'd finally close the door to her room in exasperation. And unexpectedly, my little tin of mints began disappearing daily from my nightstand. In China, Wrigley mints come in a smooth, rectangular metal container. And the kid *loved* stealing my mints. But that was also when he started falling off the bike.

We realized that Teo would bike into my room to grab the mints, but then struggle to bike while grasping the tin box in his small hand. Once unstable, our boy would tip over and land painfully, headfirst, on the floor. So, we decided he could have the mint box, as long as he kept it in his "mint bag"—a small pouch we tied to his bike. Well, this just took his glee to a whole new level for him!

Teo's day started with breakfast, after I'd already left for work. Then Minki would help him mount his bike, and the boy would come straight to my bedside table for the mints. He'd carefully place them in his mint bag and wheel off to his next adventure. I still remember being at work and glancing at my phone as Minki texted me photos of Teo chortling with exultation as he biked off with his booty.

It was around this time that our family started talking seriously about adopting Teo. We had journeyed with him for a few years now. And going from simply needing a quiet place to pass to becoming mobile, and now firmly establishing himself as a part of our family, Teo had taught us to simply go where the adventure led. For the past twelve months, we had been meeting with potential adoptive families. At one point, Teo even moved out to live with an interested couple. But after a few false starts, we began to wonder, "Is this it? Will our spare room forever be filled?"

Our family began the arduous adoption process in China, while also seeking to find his birth parents to ensure that they didn't want him back. Well, we eventually connected with them and confirmed that they were all right with our proceeding with the adoption.

So, we continued on. Minki and I traveled to the U.S., meeting a series of adoption counselors and medical advisors as the government conducted background checks. Now, as I look back at the long and complex process, one day stands out in particular.

We met an international adoptions specialist, an experienced physician who had helped countless families in our situation. She took one look at Teo's CAT scan and, with the best of intentions, sought to gently recalibrate our expectations. The doctor told us that Teo's brain had been ravaged by all the pressure in his head. Where we would normally expect to see a big, healthy organ, Teo's skull was largely empty—with the remaining parts of his brain smashed against the sides of his skull. She warned us that he could not understand us and would never be able to speak. She told us that Teo likely would never have the balance to walk...that he'd never read...or go to school.

Minki and I sat silently at the table, utterly confused. We stumbled over one another, anxious to explain how much Teo was already able to say and do. The doctor sadly shook her head and stated that with the CAT scans laid out in front of us, there was simply no way any of this was possible. She explained that we were seeing only what we wanted to see, because we loved him.

A few hours later, Minki and I were nibbling half-heartedly at our dinner in a restaurant when I finally broke the silence. I didn't know how or why Teo defied what science told us, but we knew what we knew! I declared to my husband that I believed Teo would be able to eventually stand unassisted, and that he would one day be able to walk. My courageous, tenderhearted husband agreed.

We paid our bill and wandered out into the warm summer evening. From across the parking lot, the bright blue lights of Toys "R" Us beckoned invitingly to us. And without a word, we headed towards the cheerfully lit store. There, we found a complicated jewelry-making kit we knew Laini would love, and then my eye was caught by a children's golf set on display. I thought about how Teo loved slotting his mint box into that little mint bag. About how his favorite toy was a plastic cube with cutout shapes. He spent hours pushing the right shape into the right hole. Wouldn't our little guy just love golf? Putting a ball right into a perfectly shaped hole seemed like just the thing for him.

That dusky evening, we bought the golf set. We bought it knowing what our son was capable of, and being intimately aware of the activities that captivated his interest. We bought it believing that he would be able to stand and hold a club one day. We bought it as a statement of our faith.

Shortly after we returned to China, Teo took his first step with a walker.

His determination and perseverance were nothing short of inspiring. I can still picture him taking one laborious step after another, muttering to himself as he battled his way across the floor, "Stop. Sit. *No.* Go! Stop. Go." As with everything else, he never gave up. Our boy was walking.

Yet, though we had been matched to him for final adoption, Teo wasn't yet ours on paper. Without a passport, we couldn't enroll him in school or even take him with us to the U.S. for the Christmas holiday. Instead, as we prepared to fly to America for the 2015 holidays, just as we had in 2014, the nonprofit that had brought him to our home years ago now helped us arrange for Teo to stay with another family in its network.

— · —

The timing was perfect, as a new young couple, Jackie and Jason McClure, had just signed up to open their home for a temporary childcare situation. We transitioned Teo to their home and, from across the ocean, received daily videos of him; Jackie and Jason were absolutely wonderful! They treated him like a teachable boy, not like a disabled kid or, worse, as we'd seen some do in the past, like a plant to be watered and then left alone facing a window. So, upon our return in the new year, we invited the McClures to our home for dinner as a way to thank them for taking such good care of our boy.

The doorbell rang just as we were setting the table for dinner that evening, and as Jackie and Jason stepped into our foyer, Teo, the little boy who had called me "Mama" for years, squealed in delight and loudly yelled, "Mama!" to Jackie. He army-tadpole-crawled at record speed to the door and threw his arms around her calves.

Jackie threw a concerned glance at me, but unable to restrain herself, scooped Teo up and cuddled him close. She carried him over to the dinner table, where my little boy sat next to her. He wrapped the four fingers of his left hand tightly around her right index finger, where they stayed fixed through the entire meal.

This was an absolute first for Teo. His physical and emotional reaction to this family simply couldn't be ignored. It raised a million questions and, I must admit, also planted a profound, painful ache somewhere deep inside.

Over the next few weeks, our families met frequently, and we even agreed to celebrate Chinese New Year together, sharing adjoining rooms at one of my company's hotels. We began calling ourselves the McChang family, united by the little boy we all loved.

Eventually, through hours of discussion, tears, and prayer, Minki and I decided to transfer guardianship to the McClures. It was one of the most difficult decisions we had ever made. But we knew that the younger couple loved him deeply and was prepared to support Teo with the lifetime of care he needed. Even better, they were willing to immediately take him to the States, where he would be able to access better healthcare.

We marveled at where that first step in 2012 had brought us, realizing that when we're living out our social legacy, we don't need to assume or plan for a specific outcome. In fact, contrary to my personality, I learned to flow with Teo's story as it unfolded. In 2015, our last year together, we had been prepared to adopt our sweet boy and give him a forever home, but then we realized that we were intended to play only a smaller role in his recovery. To care for him on one leg of his journey.

We also learned that as parents, we have an opportunity to adjust the way we see our roles. Our children are not a manifestation of us, or of whom we had hoped to become. They are not a reflection of our personal success or failure. Rather, we are granted, for a time, the great and humbling privilege of caring for them. Our job is to help them learn the world around them and set them up for success as global citizens. Caring for Teo helped me become a better mother to Laini and the subsequent children who stayed in our spare room.

Further, living with Teo once again reinforced to me that we are capable of infinitely more than we might imagine. Had I been asked to care for a differently abled boy for an extended period of time, much less to adopt him, I certainly would have resisted. I wouldn't have thought our family had the capacity for such an undertaking. But we had to say yes only to a few days, and then we said yes to helping him recover from his surgery. Then to supporting him as he discovered the world around him. Then as he began crawling. And then as he took his first step. We needed to say yes only to the initial ask, and then the rest unfolded as we discovered what we were really capable of.

Today, Teo lives happily with Jackie and Jason. He is thriving with his new family and loves his two little sisters. We see them as often as we can and are still overwhelmed with emotion when he refers to us as "Dada," "Mama," "Emmy," and "*jie-jie*."

In fact, I have a recent story to share with you. In 2018, our family moved to Seattle, where I accepted a temporary assignment as Senior Vice President of Marketing for Starbucks. Do you know what moved with us? The little golf toy. That box, which had sat in the back of a closet for years, was more than a little beat up, but it traveled with us across the ocean to Seattle years after we had purchased it. When we visited Teo and his family for spring break, we carried that box onto one last plane and brought it to him. He is now walking unassisted, and can swing the putter like a pro.

The Two Misters
Washington State, 2016

The idea of taking a first step into a social legacy can be either intimidating or thrilling. But while it might look like a major investment in a little boy in one instance, it can also manifest in smaller, equally powerful moments. In fact, Thomas and his leftovers sparked the idea for this entire chapter when he shared with me his story of "The Two Misters."

"You got three choices. You can be the villain, the victim, or the hero. So, which one are you?"

Seated on an overturned milk crate, Thomas took in his surroundings as he pondered the question. The tent community was littered with trash; the man seated in front of him was dressed in torn, soiled clothing. Given the context, it was impossible to consider himself a victim. "I guess I'm not really the victim. I'm for sure not going to be the villain. So how can I be the hero?"

As the moon rose over Seattle's skyline, Thomas talked through his day's frustrations with James. Having started the conversation complaining about a client he'd lost to an aggressive peer, the twenty-seven-year-old Sales Manager had indeed assumed the role of victim. Now under the frank tutelage of a man twenty-five years his senior, he reshaped his attitude towards the situation. "Thanks, Mr. James. You always give me the perspective I need," he said.

The older man laughed good-naturedly and said, "Boy, you keep feeding my belly, I do my best to feed your soul!"

Thomas stood up and brushed off his pants. "I'll see you tomorrow, Mr. James. You stay warm!" Smiling, he continued down the street as he strolled past the rest of the tent community, to where his Honda Accord was parked. As he tightened his seat belt, the young man thought back to the day he first met his unlikely friend and counselor.

— . —

Three months prior, his team had kicked off the workday with the much-anticipated weekly ritual they had playfully dubbed "breakfast happy hour." One of his five boisterous Sales Associates brought doughnuts or bagels every Friday morning, while Thomas brewed coffee for the team. As the afternoon wore on, folks would stop by the common area to nibble at the remains of breakfast, but inevitably at the end of the day, a few uneaten morsels remained on the parchment paper. That evening as the young man slid his laptop into his backpack and prepared to head home, four leftover bagels and an unopened tub of cream cheese caught his eye. Quickly wrapping the remains in paper, Thomas tucked them under his arm as he walked out the door.

He took a deep breath as the warm summer air welcomed him that evening. Thomas was relieved to discover that it wasn't raining—he had left his umbrella in the car that morning. On the other hand, the clear weather likely meant that those in the lively tent community were milling around. The quarter-mile-long homeless encampment was positioned between his office and parking lot, so he steeled himself for the half-mile walk to the car. A few of his coworkers had told stories of muggings, but in his eighteen months, the Sales Manager had never met any trouble. Walking straight and fast, Thomas had learned to navigate the periphery of the community with ease. On that Friday, he looked about, wondering what to do with the bagels tucked under his arm.

"Hey, boy!" a hoarse voice shouted at Thomas. Slowing his stride slightly, the young man respectfully replied, "Good evening, sir." The guffaw he received in response slowed his pace even more. "I ain't no sir!" the man said. "You can call me mister!"

Thomas smiled as he turned to face the man. His smile widened when he realized there were two men seated side by side, playing a game with a deck of tattered cards. Leaning forward in his threadbare folding chair, the other player hooted loudly as he shouted, "Gin!" He slapped his cards down on the plastic crate and turned to Thomas. "You call *him* mister, you call *me* mister, too. We *two misters*!" With that, the two men laughed uproariously, and Thomas joined in. Suddenly he remembered the food under his arm. "Hey, two misters," he offered, "I had extra bagels tonight I didn't know what to do with. Would you be willing to take them off my hands?"

— • —

And that's how an unlikely friendship began between Thomas, James, and André. From that first step of handing over a few bagels, the young manager began collecting leftovers from breakfast happy hour and looking for the two campers every Friday evening. As the men became better acquainted that summer, Thomas also learned more about the circumstances that had brought them to the community he walked by twice a day. Although, he remembered ruefully, the first time he'd sought to satisfy his curiosity about homelessness, James had jerked his head in displeasure. With an affronted expression, he'd stated in his gravelly voice, "I ain't *homeless*. I just don't have me a home at the present moment!"

Thomas learned that there was a difference between the chronic homeless, those who had been living on the streets for years, and the episodically displaced, those who had lost their homes for a time. "See them?" James asked, pointing at a clump of unconscious campers, one lying with a needle still protruding from his arm. "*They* homeless. They done give up—this all they *ever* gonna know."

As a longtime homeowner, James emphatically rejected the label. For most of his life, the steadfast husband and father had faithfully paid his mortgage with income from his job as a truck driver, raising his two kids in the same comfortable three-bedroom home. But after the kids had graduated and moved east for work, his wife, Sheila, became seriously ill. To cover her medical expenses, James had taken on longer-haul trips. In fact, he had driven so many overtime hours that by the time Sheila gave in to cancer after a two-year battle, he had developed severe neck and back pain from the physical stress of those long, bone-jarring rides and cramped sleeping quarters. "Doc said I couldn't drive no more, so I told the company I needed a desk job," he told Thomas. "Thought I could be a dispatcher, but they fired me instead. Told me I took unapproved home time for Sheila's funeral. After all those years, can you believe that?"

Thomas tried to imagine being in his friend's position. Ignoring the excruciating pain in his back, James would drive seventy hours in an eight-day period, spend a day and a half at home caring for his increasingly frail wife, then turn around and do it again. As Sheila's health continued to decline, he struggled to pay the mounting hospital bills, never pausing to have his own broken body examined. Then, after he buried his wife of twenty-six years, the company fired him. Unable to find another job and drowning in debt, James found himself on the street when the bank foreclosed on his house. How could a man take so many agonizing hits and still remain standing? With renewed respect, Thomas apologized and, in a respectful tone, promised to never again refer to his friend as homeless.

"Now don't you start pitying me, boy," James told him. "Even if someone done me wrong, I *ain't* no victim."

"No, sir. Mr. James, it's clear to me that you're a *hero*," James responded with quiet conviction.

At this, the older man gave a snort. He didn't speak again, but Thomas thought he caught a pleased gleam in his friend's eye.

— • —

Back at the office, Thomas's team frequently found themselves working late as fall, their busiest season, approached. By then, everyone had heard about the two misters, and breakfast happy hour was often delivered with a few extra bagels set aside for the men. Sometimes, as Thomas returned to his desk near the end of the day, he found boxes of food at his desk labeled "for the two misters" with sticky notes.

One fall evening, Thomas took a seat on an upturned bucket to chat with the two misters, exhausted after a long week. Leaning back against their two side-by-side tents, James closed his eyes, blissfully sinking his teeth into a glazed Top Pot doughnut. André, sitting in his usual spot alongside his friend, picked up a jelly-filled one and thanked Thomas for his thoughtfulness. "Young man, our crew took down one of the biggest trees I've ever seen today. I am bone-tired, and this is just what I needed." Surprised, the young Sales Manager leaned forward, resting his elbows on his knees. "Mr. André, I didn't know you had a job."

André chuckled at Thomas's astonished expression when he declared that more than half of those living in the tent community held regular jobs; he had worked on a grounds crew for years. "Boy, we ain't here cuz we're deadbeats. I been working hard *all* my life. Just don't make enough to rent my own place no more."

André recalled the day he'd been evicted. Returning home after a hard day's work dragging brush and lifting heavy wood rounds, he had wearily climbed the steps to his apartment and nearly missed seeing the notice taped to the door. His landlord had stuck a no-cause notice on his door, giving the resident just twenty days to vacate his home. That evening, he and his wife frantically called friends and relatives, trying to understand their dire circumstances. "Landlord don't need to give a reason for 'no cause.' We didn't get out in twenty days, he'd bring us to court," the man told Thomas with a resigned voice.

Thomas was stunned. He pulled out his phone and began to google Washington state residential laws as André continued reliving his story. With their marriage already struggling after two painful miscarriages, his wife had packed her bags that same day and moved in with her sister. The next two weeks passed in a confusing whirlwind, and then André found himself on the streets, all his belongings stuffed in the same two American Tourister suitcases he had bought years ago for their honeymoon. Listening to the story, Thomas couldn't comprehend how a landlord could just oust a tenant like that. But scrolling on his phone, he realized that André was far from alone. Frowning, Thomas read that between 2006 and 2017, the mean Seattle residential rental cost had risen from $1,017 to $1,443 a month. That meant while the average renter in 2006 had needed an annual salary of $72,256 to make the median rent, a renter in 2017 needed $102,522.[2] In fact, in 2017, nearly half of households that rented in the Seattle metro area were considered "housing cost burdened," meaning they spent more than 30 percent of their income on rent alone. Suddenly, it made sense why so many campers were living rough, though they maintained a steady income with full-time work.

"Mr. André, I had no idea. Man, that must have been the worst few weeks of your life!" Thomas blurted out passionately.

"Son, that wasn't the worst part. I tell you what, a few months later, some fool started a fire near my tent. I lost most of my clothes, my cookstove, all my food. Thank God I had my wallet in my pocket!" Then he somberly said, "Every time I hit a new low, the carpet got pulled from under me and I done fall even lower. How's a man supposed to get up from all that?" Thomas could only shake his head in silence.

As Thomas's friendship with the two misters continued to develop, his sympathy for their situation continued to deepen. He began collecting blankets and clothing for the guys. One weekend on a whim, he bought a Marvel superhero camping chair to replace James's rickety old folding chair. With a Sharpie marker, he carefully wrote on the back, "You can be the villain, the victim, or the hero. So, which one are you?"

— · —

Those Friday evening chats became a cherished part of Thomas's weekly routine. And as winter approached, he began to microwave the misters' food before heading outside. Rain or shine, the three men sat huddled, catching up on the week. By the end of November, James had developed a deep, hacking cough that racked the man's body with such force, it sometimes took his breath away. He waved away Thomas's concerns and refused to see a doctor: "It ain't nothing serious. I'm still 'plassing.' You think they take my blood if I got something wrong?"

From a previous conversation, Thomas knew about James's "plassing." James gave blood plasma as often as he could, earning forty dollars for each donation; it was his only means of collecting income. Now seeing his friend's unease around the topic of his health, Thomas shifted the conversation to a more positive note. "Hey, guys, I've got a date with Tamara next week. She's coming by the office before we go to dinner downtown. Can I bring her by to meet you?" The two men were elated at the idea of meeting their boy's new love interest. They were still chattering excitedly about it as Thomas headed home for the weekend.

That week passed quickly, as downtown decorations reminded Thomas that the holidays were fast approaching. Growing increasingly nervous the following week as he and Tamara neared the tent community, Thomas reiterated, "Tam, they only have like two changes of clothing and no showers. Are you sure you're ready for this?" Despite her lighthearted reassurances, Thomas wiped sweaty palms on the thighs of his jeans and looked around nervously. He really liked Tamara, but they'd only recently started dating and he didn't want to scare her off.

Then, a massive smile spread across his face when she pulled a ten-pack of hand warmers from her purse. Striding purposefully toward the two men who were already yelling her boyfriend's name, Tamara reached the two misters first. "You must be André and James," she said. Shaking their hands firmly, she continued warmly, "I've heard so much about you! I was hoping you could use these; I had some extra at work."

The two misters gleefully shook out the hand warmers, slipping the packets inside their gloves. "Son, she's a keeper! Ooh, that hit the spot! Where you work, Tamara?"

She explained that she worked in the merchandising department at REI out in Kent, a forty-minute drive from Seattle. Thomas slung his arm around Tamara, saying, "That's why downtown dinner dates are a special occasion for us."

"Well, you kids better get going then!" James rasped. "And our dinner here's getting cold. We see you next week, Thomas."

The two older men hungrily unwrapped their meal as the young couple headed towards the car.

The next Friday, Thomas was already out the door when he realized that he didn't have any food for his friends. The office had been crazy as folks rushed to wrap things up before the holidays. That morning, a team member had forgotten to bring food for breakfast happy hour. And now, Thomas was already running late to dinner with Tamara out in Kent.

But seeing his breath cloud before him as the door swung open gave him pause. Thomas's mind immediately went to James and André, likely wrapped in blankets and huddled in their tents on a cold night like this one. The young manager turned to badge back into the office building and ran over to the vending machine. Five minutes later, balancing two steaming Cup-a-Soup containers, Thomas backed his way through the door and once again stepped out onto the street.

As expected, the two misters were zipped into a tent, but he heard their familiar voices even as he approached. "Hey, guys! Open up before I spill this soup!" he called out. After a quick hello, Thomas explained about dinner at Tamara's house and rushed to his car.

The next two days flew by all too quickly. Thomas had ended up spending his weekend in Kent, and floated back to work on Monday in a happy haze. He looked forward to telling the two misters about his weekend, and also wanted to ask their advice on the Christmas gift he'd purchased for Tamara. The smitten man wondered if the Diptyque candle set he'd selected was personal enough. The guys would definitely have advice—"Probably too *much* advice," he thought with a fond smile.

That evening, though it wasn't a Friday, Thomas picked up some falafel from the food truck across the street and made his way towards the tents. As his eyes flicked from left to right, Thomas noticed that the community seemed unusually subdued. He shook off a sense of foreboding, remembering that these days, the sun went down just after four o'clock and most campers were already bundled inside their tents, the fuzzy glow of their mobile devices visible from the road.

But as Thomas neared the two misters' space, his sense of disquiet quickly elevated to alarm. Instead of the usual outline of two tents, only one hump was visible against the sapphire night sky. James's tent looked like it had been pillaged, the tent poles lying broken on the ground. His red sleeping bag had been yanked through the unzipped opening, giving the grotesque appearance of a twisted, oversized tongue. "James! André! What's going on?!" Thomas shouted in alarm as his hands anxiously crushed the warm box of food.

He waited impatiently, shifting his weight from one foot to the other, as André's tent slowly unzipped. The older man looked shaky and haggard as he slowly stepped out into the cold. He peered at Thomas with red-rimmed eyes, a gloved hand wearily rubbing the back of his neck.

"He didn't want you to know, Thomas. James had lung cancer. He been struggling more and more, this cold weather doing him no good."

Thomas recalled that nasty rattling cough and the cigarette hanging from the corner of James's mouth, like a permanent fixture on his careworn face. He said nothing, his shoulders slumping as the unexpected tragedy sank in.

André continued, "On Saturday, his one leg got real swollen. Seems the cancer thickened his blood and he got himself a clot." Thomas later learned that deep vein thrombosis is often fatal if the clot breaks free from leg veins and makes its way to the heart. It is also the next leading cause of death in cancer patients after cancer itself.

André went on: "You know, son, that soup you brought us on Friday was the last warm meal James had." Thomas's throat tightened painfully as he listened. "I know you was in a hurry, but you took that extra time to feed us ole misters. And it sure meant a lot."

"I should have done more," the grief-stricken man choked out. "I knew the winter was too cold. I should have found you guys a better shelter!"

André slowly shuffled over to Thomas, resting a heavy hand on his shoulder. "Thomas, it ain't about *shelter*. This our *community*. Community what kept him alive. And *you*. You became part of that community. You done good. You done right by James."

Taking comfort from André's warm embrace, Thomas thought back to Friday night. He had nearly run out the door without taking any food for the two misters. Suddenly overwhelmed with gratitude that he had turned back around, he reflected on how he would be feeling right now if he hadn't brought those hot soups out.

Taking a deep breath, he thought back to how the unlikely relationship had blossomed, all beginning with that first step nearly half a year before. As he glanced at the superhero camping chair lying on the ground, Thomas read his own handwriting: "You got three choices. You can be the villain, the victim, or the hero. So, which one are you?"

The Vacation
Utila, Honduras, 2015

The stunning young blond woman grimaced as her flip-flop sank into the thick, murky water. Gingerly extracting her shoe out of the gray-green sludge, Allison looked around the ghetto that was called Campenado. "How on earth did my life end up bringing me here?" she mused incredulously.

Allison had grown up in a posh home on the Upper East Side of Manhattan with her parents and four siblings. As she developed a taste for fashion, the petite teenager was often spotted in the season's hottest collections. To round out the fairy tale, when Allison was admitted to Rhode Island School of Design, it seemed inevitable that she would achieve her aspiration of becoming a fashion designer.

Yet, just a few years later, the trajectory of Allison's life took an unexpected turn. In their twenties, she and her boyfriend, Zach, best friends since they were seven years old, had decided to take a Caribbean vacation. Seeking the world's most beautiful scuba diving, the couple flew to a small island called Utila, off the coast of Honduras.

There, after just a few days on the charming but primitive island, the couple had become accustomed to its simple, unhurried pace. They rented a golf cart to get around, because the uneven dirt roads made carts and scooters the only practical mode of local transportation. They learned to identify key milestones, because an address system had yet to be developed on the beach. Instead of looking for numbers, they soon became familiar with "the blue house," "Seabreeze House at the point," and "the bar on Pumpkin Hill."

And after sampling the smattering of restaurants and bars available, the couple soon began returning to their favorite hot spots for repeat meals. One evening, looking as if she'd just stepped out of the pages of *Vanity Fair*, Allison approached the now familiar entrance to Skid Row Bar & Grill as Zach parked the cart. She paused to gaze sympathetically at an old dog seated in his usual spot on the porch. "Where are all your friends, bud?" she asked the mutt as she leaned against the railing and waited for Zach.

Then, feeling his hand on the small of her back, she turned to smile at her boyfriend. "What are you doing, babe?" he asked, gently pulling her away. "You're allergic to cats and dogs!"

Allison allowed herself to be led toward the doorway and responded, "I know. I don't even *like* animals. But there's something about that guy. Did you see the way he looked at me?"

Heading inside, the couple was soon seated at a corner table. And when the server overheard Allison refer to the old dog's wise, knowing eyes, she chimed in. "Ah, you met Bingo!" the young woman exclaimed. "He *does* have the most soulful eyes! You know, we always chase away the strays at the door, but we let that old guy hang out. He's a total sweetheart."

That evening, though her burger was perfectly seasoned, Allison asked for a to-go box and packed up half her meal. Stepping back outside, relaxed in the velvety smoothness of a good bottle of wine, she opened the cardboard box and offered her remains to old Bingo.

Driving back to their hotel that night, Zach glanced at his girlfriend, perplexed. "Well, that was different," he commented. Seated beside him as they bounced across the bumpy terrain, Allison simply flashed him a drowsy, winsome smile.

The next day, Allison returned to Skid Row to feed Bingo another meal. Soon, the old, toothless dog's wiry tail began to thump as he watched his benefactress cross the street with his daily meal in hand. With renewed perspective, the American girl began noticing the island's many malnourished strays. Many exhibited signs of abuse and neglect, and all of them seemed magnetically drawn to her.

The couple's vacation passed quickly and, on the day before they were scheduled to fly home, the sophisticated city girl, elegantly perched on her towel at the beach across from Skid Row, was seen holding court with an odd, bedraggled collection of creatures. Bingo was seated staunchly beside her and staring lovingly into her eyes, while a motley crew idled quietly nearby. Gazing sadly at the scruffy, pitiful animals, Allison realized that all of these dogs would soon die without medical attention.

Then, she was struck by a wonderful epiphany. These dogs needed help, and the islanders could use education on how to care for the animals. They could benefit from learning to neuter and spay the dogs to control the population. These were things she could help with, and she suddenly realized that she would have to come back to the island.

"Babe, we've already established that you don't like animals, and even more, you're allergic to them!" Zach exclaimed, staring at his girlfriend in bewilderment.

Allison laughed happily. "I know!" she responded. "But I can take allergy medicine. And *this* is what I want to do. Zach, I want to come back to Utila and start giving these animals the care they deserve."

"What about fashion design?" her boyfriend asked.

"Suddenly, faced with all these sad, adorable, amazing animals who need my help, it seems like a preposterously shallow career," Allison said simply.

"OK," Zach responded slowly, "but what's your endgame? Do you really think you can help *all* the animals on the island?"

Seemingly unconcerned, Allison replied, "I don't think I need an endgame right now. We'll take it one step at a time and just see where it goes."

— • —

A few months later, Allison and Zach settled into their new home on the island of Utila. Though he was happy to return to the beautiful island, Zach secretly agreed with his girlfriend's parents; this was likely just a phase, and the tiresome, thankless work of caring for strays would soon bore the vivacious young woman.

But Allison's energy didn't flag at all in their first few months. She had returned to Utila ready to tackle the animals' needs, galvanized by a new purpose. The New Yorker traded her four-inch stilettos for rubber flip-flops and worked seventeen-hour days in the relentless heat, investing her own money to begin neutering and spaying the many strays. Importing basic medical supplies, she also nursed injured street dogs back to health.

The island, which had never housed a full-time animal vet or shelter, was in dire need of help. So, word spread quickly in the small community, and soon many islanders began bringing their dogs to Allison...dogs who had been hit by a car, who suffered from heartworm, or who needed to be neutered. Over the next two years, Allison happily took care of them all.

"You can't keep up this pace," Zach protested one day. He watched as his exhausted girlfriend dragged herself into the shower after another grueling day. "I know you don't have an endgame, but taking care of these animals one at a time is just nuts! You need help."

Later that day, his words rang in Allison's head as she flew on a chartered flight to La Ceiba, on the mainland of Honduras, with a few dogs that needed more medical care than she could provide. Allison knew that Zach was right. And a short half day later, the refreshed woman returned to the island, buzzing with excitement over her new solution. One of the vet technicians at the La Ceiba veterinarian clinic had been impressed by what she was trying to do for Utila. The tech was from World Vets, an international veterinary aid organization, and had treated hundreds of animals; she was enthralled by the idea of building something from scratch with Allison. She had agreed to come to Utila, bringing a wealth of knowledge and experience with her to the island.

The two women bought a golf cart to efficiently visit their many patients across the small landmass. Filling two suitcases with supplies, the partners worked from this mobile care unit for the better part of the next year. Hundreds of dogs benefited from them and the soon infamous golf cart. More importantly, the islanders began to learn about proper pet care. Soon, her grateful patients' donations began to supplement Allison's personal investment, and local volunteers stepped up to help.

Yet in spite of the momentum, the New Yorker once again found herself dreaming about the next thing. Secure in her Offer and knowing she was making a difference, she now realized that she needed a stable location to house strays, helping prevent disease and injury, as well as a pleasant space to facilitate adoptions of rehabilitated animals. Never having dreamed she would build her own animal shelter, the woman who was allergic to cats and dogs began to sketch her ideas. And with the help of local volunteers, a community space was soon erected and immediately filled.

Jasper's Utila Animal Shelter took nearly a year to build, and in the meantime, Allison continued to work from her golf cart and expand her staff. Now, three committed partners often made house calls, rushing to help islanders when animals were too injured or sick to be moved.

They worked feverishly, rarely stopping to enjoy the vibrant social life on the island. But one evening after a particularly long week, the ladies allowed themselves a well-deserved break and dressed to go out, to enjoy some rare time off at Allison's favorite bar, Skid Row. Allison was still sipping her first glass of wine when she received an urgent text. Her kohl-rimmed eyes widened for a moment when she saw that the emergency was in Campenado, a grungy, swampy ghetto on the other side of the island. But armed with their supplies and driven by a burning sense of purpose, the fashionable former urbanite and her partners, in their cocktail dresses, raced to help.

As she drove the golf cart across mounds of slimy trash, Allison could make out a giant Honduran man looming in front of her, a black silhouette against the harsh glare of her headlights. A tiny ramshackle hut teetered behind him, looking far too small to shelter the enormous man. Suddenly glad to have brought her team with her, Allison murmured quietly, "Andrea, make sure you have Zach on speed dial...just in case."

But as she stepped out of the cart and approached the man, her eyes were drawn to a tiny, limp puppy held tenderly in the man's large hands. That evening, the ladies' cocktail dresses sparkled in the blaze of their cart's headlights as they started an IV right there on the unpaved road. Extending a meaty hand that completely enveloped Allison's own, the grateful man introduced himself: "*Gracias*. I'm Saul" (pronounced "sah-ool").

The next day, Allison braved the swampy muck once again, retracing the previous evening's route to check on Saul's puppy. Now, in the sweltering afternoon sun, she noticed small, dirty faces peering at her from between panels of rusted tin walls. A diapered baby lay listlessly on the filthy ground, no adult in sight. And a few feet away, what appeared to be a dead dog lay half submerged in a scummy pond, flies buzzing greedily around the body. In the light of day, Campenado was even more appalling. But Allison saw it only as the next stage in the evolution of her social legacy; she had started her work individually, then organized a mobile unit, and eventually hired staff. Now, Allison set her sights on the ghetto as her next big challenge.

Soon, she began bringing supplies and medicine into Campenado. Though she spoke fluent Spanish and knew the area well, the petite woman felt reassured every time Saul joined her on these trips. On the day her flip-flop had gotten sucked into the muddy swamp between boards that served as an impromptu walking path, the pair had been preparing to transport a German shepherd named Dorothy back to the shelter. Chained up around the clock, the dog was wretched and emaciated, and began shivering uncontrollably as soon as any person approached her. Her owner, Carlos, was a frequent drug user, renowned in Campenado for his violent, erratic behavior. Yet, feeling sentimental one day, he had called down to Allison through the open window: "Hey, you can take her if you fix her hip. That dog can't walk no more!"

Allison's compassionate eyes lit up with joy as she leaned down toward the dog, whispering conspiratorially, "You hear that? I'm coming back to get you tomorrow." So, the next day, with Saul's help, the young woman, now barefoot, drove a trembling Dorothy back to the shelter. And after a couple of months of good food, tender love, and an osteotomy to relieve hip pain, the big dog had become the shelter's cheerful mascot. She followed Allison everywhere and greeted visitors with delight.

So, the shelter's staff could only stare in dismay when, one afternoon, Dorothy jumped to her feet and began to growl. Stiff-legged, the large dog snarled menacingly as she stalked toward the door. Her unusual behavior was soon explained when a familiar unhinged voice sang out, "That's my dog! I'm here to take her back. Need me some target practice!"

Allison raced from the treatment room as soon as she heard Carlos's shaky voice. The man was clearly high, staggering as he reached for Dorothy. Allison stepped between man and dog. "I didn't rehabilitate her so you could shoot her! Get out of here!" she shouted, eyes blazing.

Over the next few weeks, Carlos repeatedly returned to the shelter, unwashed; he threatened to kill Allison if she didn't hand over the dog. One day, wide-eyed, he charged into the shelter and screamed that he would burn the building to the ground. She refused to be intimidated, and engaged first the police, then the mayor. While laws are lax on the island, Allison is now petitioning for the police to take a more active role in known animal abuse cases. Along with the Carlos situation, she is calling attention to a man who slaughtered his neighbor's entire litter of puppies, and another who attacks strays with a machete for sport. While those discussions continue, today Dorothy remains safely at the shelter.

The petite blonde dynamo who visited Utila on vacation five years ago now calls the island home. Jasper's Utila Animal Shelter is thriving, benefiting from a new, experienced veterinarian on board. At just thirty-three years of age, Allison has faced death threats and stood her ground against intimidating drug dealers. She braves the toughest ghettos to care for the community. Slowly, the stray population is being managed down in partnership with the local islanders. And Allison, now more beautiful than ever, couldn't imagine herself anywhere else.

—REFLECTION—

Now that you have defined your social legacy, are you ready to take your first step? In this chapter, whether it is a baby left to die, some extra bagels, or a Caribbean vacation, each story provides a glimpse of how one small step can lead to an extraordinary impact. But it requires courage, not only to take that first step but to journey on the path as it unfolds—especially for more planful, controlling types (like me!).

Here are five considerations to help you get started.

- **Anchor.** Ground yourself in your social legacy. Write it out and place it somewhere you'll see at the beginning and end of each day. Consider writing it on your bathroom mirror with a glass pen, or on a sticky note for your car dashboard. If you're more digitally oriented, make it your mobile home screen or your computer screensaver.

> *What if nothing were insignificant?*
>
> *What if everything happened for a reason? Whether or not you already believe this to be true, how would having the mindset affect the way you see the world?*
>
> *Where might you detect an opportunity or prompt to take a first step toward your social legacy?*

- **Balance.** Whether your first step will be a large one or a small one, are you starting from a sure-footed position? Referring back to the nonnegotiable elements you identified in Chapter One, are you physically, financially, emotionally, and spiritually grounded? If not, determine the source of your asymmetry and adjust before moving forward.
- **Energize.** The concept of activation energy refers to the minimum energy needed for a chemical reaction to occur.

Intuitively, bigger desired reactions require more activation energy. So, consider the magnitude of your first step and ensure you have adequate fuel to begin. As you do, remember, you're not signing up for a marathon; the first step is just a short sprint and you're committed only to the point of your choosing.

- **Flex.** Flex capacity is all about buffer. Refer back to Chapter One, which categorizes available resources as time, energy, and material wealth. Now, consider your social legacy and define what a first step might look like. Are your resources time and space, which we provided for Teo? Or do you possess a physical resource, like the food Thomas supplied to the two misters? Does it take the shape of Allison's social legacy in Utila, which first and foremost required energy and commitment? Do you have the flex capacity needed in the right area to get started?

- **Pause.** As you embark on your first step, don't forget to stop and reflect. Expect your life to be enriched, and look for this enrichment. As Thomas developed his friendship with James and André, he found in them two valuable life mentors, even as his own worldview expanded and evolved. My husband, daughter, and I, in our more challenging moments with Teo, reminded one another to pause and appreciate the joy that our boy brought to our lives.

Now, you may feel anchored and balanced but remain concerned that you don't have the activation energy or flex capacity. Perhaps you're already engaging in positive activities today. Consider this: might those good things be holding you back from the great? If this is resonating with you, take some time and examine your priorities today.

Maybe putting aside one of those "good" prerogatives will free up capacity to invest in something "great." Are there any tasks you're performing that others might be able to do equally well? And might there be something else you're uniquely positioned to do that no one else could accomplish but you? The table below can help you identify the possibilities.

> **What's your wind factor?**
>
> *Our family has recently started playing badminton. As a lifelong tennis player, I love racquet sports. But as we've been playing this new game in our yard, I have realized that wind factor has substantial impact on my performance.*
>
> *What's the wind factor in your life? What element of uncertainty could threaten to blow you off course? If you're able to anticipate it, you might mitigate its impact and stay on track.*

Priority	Impact	Passion	Growth
What am I spending time and energy on today?	How much does this priority change the world?	How much does this activity energize me?	How much does this work help me grow as a person?

Figure 4.1

Are you still feeling hesitant? Consider this: What's the worst that can happen? Construe an exit plan. Allison could have headed back to New York at any time, and Thomas could have passed through the tent community without stopping. Concurrent to your worst-case scenario, also consider the upside. Taking a first step on a new journey will undoubtedly broaden your perspective. You will discover new expanses on the horizon that were not visible from your previous position. And it's very likely that you will open yourself up to positive development and personal growth.

Now, before moving on, please take a moment to reflect on what you have determined.

What if there were freedom in the flow?

Have you ever floated downstream, gently pulled by a river? You weren't really in control of your body, yet you were able to relax into the push and pull around you.

Our family used to "city surf," jumping on the metro and randomly exiting a new station. How often we discovered a fabulous new restaurant or a shop that sold the exact thing we'd been searching for as we explored! It was a marvelous way to become accustomed to the sensation of flowing in the everyday.

The concept of the unplanned, of surrendering to uncertainty, can be a scary one. But what if you looked at that surrender not as a head-down defeat, but rather as relaxing in the flow, the sun shining upon your face?

THE FIRST STEP I WILL TAKE TOWARD LIVING MY SOCIAL
LEGACY:

_____

_____

HOW I WILL ANCHOR MYSELF IN MY SOCIAL LEGACY:

_____

_____

HOW I'M TRACKING IN MY NONNEGOTIABLE ITEMS AND ANY
STEPS I NEED TO TAKE TO STABILIZE MY BALANCE:

_____

_____

THE "GOOD" THINGS I WILL DEPRIORITIZE TO MAKE ROOM
FOR THE "GREAT":

_____

_____

—RESOURCES—

If you would like to help or adopt babies like Teo, you can get started by checking out organizations like Holt International, at https://www.holtinternational.org/china/, or All God's ChildrenInternational,athttps://allgodschildren.org/international-adoption/adopt-china/.

If Thomas's experience with the two misters struck a chord, try doing what he did. After hearing his story, I've not been able to leave a restaurant without packing leftovers. Someone out there is hungry tonight. Otherwise, collect grocery gift cards or hand out unscented baby wipes. If you prefer something more structured, you can volunteer at an emergency shelter with an organization like Volunteers of America. Check out https://www.voa.org/volunteer to find opportunities near you.

Perhaps Allison's story resonated with you. You can visit Jasper's Utila Animal Shelter and work alongside her, bottle-feeding puppies and caring for injured animals. Adopt one of the forty cats or sixty dogs that are looking for a home, including Charlie. The thin, faded machete scars on the gorgeous tan pit bull's face now look like laugh lines, giving him the appearance of a distinguished gentleman. Connect with Allison and her team at: https://www.facebook.com/JaspersUtilaAnimalShelter/.

CHAPTER 5

The Unpaved Road

Feeling confident and purposeful in your social legacy, step out onto the unpaved road.

"Life begins at the end of your comfort zone."
—NEALE DONALD WALSCH

The Prostitute's Daughter
Shanghai, China, 2017

"Excuse me, I'm sorry for being forward. But may I ask what happened to your boy?" a tall, dark-skinned woman asked my husband, politely stopping him on the street.

Unlike many local Chinese families who hid their differently abled children, we brought Teo everywhere with us. At times, we were vilified for reprimanding him ("How beastly! That boy can't be expected to understand them") or glorified for caring for him ("You're such saints to take in that awful-looking monster"). Needless to say, seeing Teo initiated countless conversations with strangers on the street.

On this particular morning, my husband had just dropped Laini off at school and was walking back home. The woman who stopped him also dropped off her kids in the mornings, so they had become accustomed to nodding politely at each other, and she had seen him with Teo, who was now with the McClures.

My husband explained to the woman that Teo had been placed with a forever family. She expressed relief, worried that something terrible had happened to him. Then, a few weeks later, the same elegant woman approached my husband in front of Laini's school. She politely introduced herself: "Remember me? I had asked about your son. I was wondering if I might have a minute of your time." The pair crossed the street and chatted on the patio of a coffee shop for the next hour. The woman, Sharon, shared that she'd started up a nonprofit in Shanghai many years ago. And noticing that our family had been willing to take Teo in, she wondered if we might be willing to help care for one of her children, Lotus.

Before talking about Lotus, Sharon shared her personal story. Eight years prior, she had noticed a low-end brothel right around the corner from her comfortable complex, as well as small children wandering the streets looking for food and companionship while their parents worked through the evenings.

But it was the day Sharon discovered a dead baby that pushed her over the edge, from a state of curious concern to passionate, driven action. She was nearly home after dropping her kids off at school that morning. Stepping around a pile of trash in the street, she gasped when she saw an infant's small arm poking incongruously out from amid the detritus. The dismayed woman frantically pushed refuse aside to reveal a tiny, rigid corpse, still loosely wrapped in a thin blanket.

As Sharon had spent years in the country after relocating from her home in the U.K., her Chinese was fluent. And as she engaged her neighbors over the gruesome discovery, the distraught woman, a mother of three, discovered that it was not uncommon for babies to suffocate in their cribs at night while the parents were out working. Meanwhile, the older kids ran wild in the streets during the day and fended for themselves at night. Hearing these revelations served as a defining moment for the mother of three.

Sharon sprang into action, kick-starting her own social legacy. She rented a second apartment near her home and began inviting the children of night workers in for free meals. Understanding that many of the kids didn't have national identification, Sharon realized they were unable to attend school. So, over the next few years, she hired a few tutors to teach the children as well.

Over time, Sharon got to know many of the children well. She helped them with whatever they needed and often advised their parents, too. But one child in particular had captured Sharon's heart.

Lotus first came to the apartment when she was just five years old. Her mother, a prostitute who worked every evening of the week, dropped the girl off each morning, so that she could get some sleep during the day.

Lotus had been born in the brothel. Growing up, she shared a small, dirty room with her mom and countless johns. Lotus also knew her father but didn't spend much time with him, because he was her mother's pimp and, in fact, had fathered more than a few of the kids in the building.

For years, Lotus endured unspeakable abuse living in that brothel. The scars on her face and body screamed of the hell she had lived through, but the damage to her spirit was far more crippling and ran much deeper.

Yet, Lotus considered herself lucky, because her mother had bothered to register her for a *shen fen zheng*, or national identity number. This meant that Lotus was able to attend a local school. One afternoon at Sharon's apartment, Lotus thought back to her first day of school. Lotus's mother had led her across three busy streets, instructing sternly, "Watch carefully. This is how you will walk by yourself tomorrow. Wait for the light to turn green, then follow the crowd." Almost as an afterthought, she flicked these words over her shoulder: "Oh, and don't get run over by a car."

Upon hearing those words, the diminutive girl felt as if her feet had been transformed into heavy blocks of stone. Rooted to the spot, Lotus became terrified at the idea of having to cross such large, busy intersections by herself. Her mother impatiently yanked at her arm, saying, "*Guo lai!* Get over here! You cannot be late for school...imagine my embarrassment!"

Somehow Lotus found her way each morning and never missed a day of school. But she was always very tired in the morning, and the teacher often slapped the glasses right off her face for falling asleep in class.

The problem was, Lotus was unable to get a full night's sleep at the brothel. Evenings were always the building's busiest time, and the girl remembered being carried down to the bar on the ground level of their ramshackle building even as a baby. To keep Lotus from toddling off, her chubby wrist was tied to the bottom rung of a bar stool with a dirty piece of string. She remembered crying quietly on the sticky floor as a terribly prickly feeling soon burned up and down her arm, as she wriggled her hand back and forth to ease the discomfort.

A short while into each evening, when Lotus's mother found an interested customer, she would untie the string and carry the girl back upstairs. Lotus was placed on the grimy floor, and even at a young age, she knew not to make a sound until the customer had left, pulling the door shut behind him.

Sometimes, Lotus remembered lying underneath the mattress, watching the rusty springs bounce just a few times before it was over. Other times, she remembered the distressing sound of her mother's muffled screams go on and on, until Lotus finally fell asleep, curled up in the farthest corner of the room. Many years later, Lotus would visit the butcher with me, and the sound of meat being tenderized would bring horrific memories flooding back. She stood beside me in the small specialty shop, tears flooding down her cheeks as she watched the meat mallet coming down again and again on a slab of red, bleeding steak.

But Lotus didn't share these memories easily. The teen had lived with us for months before she finally began opening up.

We first met Lotus when she was thirteen years old, at a dim sum shop, where Sharon brought her to make an introduction over lunch. I still remember our family preparing for that meeting. Not having welcomed anyone from such a challenged background into our home before, we felt unprepared for what lay ahead. We asked ourselves what we might see or hear from the girl that would cause us to say no. Yet, despite feeling pushed well outside our comfort zone, we couldn't imagine experiencing anything that would cause us to turn our backs and fail to offer help to a child in need. With a deep breath, the three of us nervously entered the restaurant.

She walked in right behind us. Bundled in a thick winter jacket and smearing the fog away from her glasses, Lotus looked like an ordinary Chinese teenager. She greeted us confidently and maintained a steady conversation through the meal. Minki, Laini, and I looked at one another, sending silent questions and small nods of affirmation across the table.

Lotus certainly had a lot to say. She was opinionated and assertive and ate voraciously. But we appreciated her indomitable spirit and heartfelt earnestness. We also took confidence in having established our family's social legacy; we saw our purpose as providing sanctuary, or comforting *kibun*, to vulnerable children. So, at the end of the meal, we took the step forward and invited Lotus to move into our spare room.

— · —

As she moved in, a few surprises caught us off guard. First was the smell. As soon as Lotus unzipped her winter coat, a pungent odor assaulted us, bringing tears to my eyes. And then she took off her shoes.

The rancid smell immediately transported me back to eighth-grade biology class—that moment when my scalpel sliced smoothly through the fetal pig's skin to reveal the embalmed organs within. Looking down at Lotus's feet, I was shocked to see them coated with a thick, fuzzy layer of mold. As she followed my eyes, the girl quickly slipped her feet into a pair of slippers and shuffled towards her new room.

So, what's the protocol for bringing a stranger's child into your home? Minki and I listed the risks we were taking on. Were we risking our daughter's health, or even our own? What if something happened to this brash girl while she stayed with us? We would be accountable if she were to get hurt. How much did we trust her with Laini? What if her gangster father found out where she was living and came looking for her?

We decided to put our personal anxieties on the back burner, and instead invested our energy in helping our guest feel welcomed and accepted. Still, the hygiene issue required immediate attention. To avoid overwhelming her or causing her to feel bad, we decided to gently introduce one new thing each week.

The first week, I reassured Lotus that we wouldn't parent her, and just wanted to provide her a safe place to live. We would ensure she had three healthy meals a day and would help her get to and from school. Our only request was that she take a shower each evening when she returned to the house.

The teenage girl easily accepted this, and we were off to a great start!

That first week, Lotus and I returned home around the same time each evening. Her school ended around six p.m., and she then stayed in the building for *bu shi ban*, China's ubiquitous after-school tutoring. Meanwhile, I would return home from across town, where I was working as the chief marketing officer for Starbucks, China. We would meet in the kitchen around eight p.m., where we would eat leftovers together (Minki and Laini had eaten hours earlier). After a quick meal, Lotus would shuffle into the shower as I read a bedtime story with my daughter.

With the bathroom right across the hall from my daughter's room, we were hit with a terribly astringent odor every time Lotus finished her shower. We simply couldn't understand how the girl could come out smelling worse than when she went in. So, in the second week, I introduced Lotus to deodorant.

I told her that, in America, girls used deodorant to reduce perspiration and manage body odor. Though she surveyed my imported collection of Secret deodorant products with misgiving, the teenager selected a pale blue stick without argument.

But the smells did not improve that second week, and the stench wafting from the bathroom was only getting worse. Even more horrifying, I caught a glimpse of Lotus wrapped in a towel and saw that the black fungus now crept up her ankles, wrapping around her calves.

Laini had the revelation first: "Mom, do you think she knows *how* to shower? Did you look at the shampoo and soap? Have they been used?" I jumped up from her bed and crossed the hall into the bathroom. One glance told me that the shampoo pump was still in its originally locked position. Even the fresh bar of soap retained its sharp, powdery edges.

So, the next evening as we shared leftovers in the kitchen, I asked Lotus, "How are your showers? Are you getting used to the idea of taking one each evening?" Lotus grunted as she smacked her lips wetly while chewing. Then, instead of answering me, she loudly spit some fish bones onto the floor right by my feet.

I jumped back and exclaimed, "Lotus, why did you do that?" She looked at me blankly and asked, "Where else should I spit fish bones? It's no problem.... That's why we wear slippers." I thought of all those dinners at local Chinese restaurants where I had observed locals spitting their bones out right onto the table, or directly onto the floor. I gentled my tone and replied, "I understand that might be your habit. But in our house, because we have dogs that might choke on those bones, please deposit those bones into a napkin." Lotus guffawed and sprayed particles of food at me as she responded loudly, "What a waste of a napkin! Rich people are really too much."

I returned to the topic of the shower and asked her if she'd gotten used to the new habit. The teen squirmed a little, responding, "The mold on my legs is getting worse, and I'd rather not wash so much. But if I need to do it to keep living here, I will." Swallowing hard, I offered, "Maybe I can shower with you and show you how we clean ourselves in our family. Maybe with more soapy scrubbing, we can help improve your mold problem."

That same evening, I got into the shower with Lotus. While I was way out of my comfort zone, feeling embarrassed and self-conscious, the teenager didn't seem at all fazed by the situation or our shared nakedness. I supposed she had seen plenty of naked bodies where she used to live.

I asked Lotus to show me how she showered. She stepped directly under the water, drenched herself completely, and then turned off the faucet. I suddenly understood why the mold situation wasn't improving—we were actually cultivating it at an accelerated rate!

So, I turned the water back on and picked up the bar of soap, showing Lotus how we clean ourselves. I pumped a few pumps of shampoo and thickly lathered my hair. As she did the same, I explained the benefits of using conditioner, the second bottle on the shelf. The bathroom immediately filled with the pleasant fragrance of Pantene haircare products.

We toweled ourselves off and I tried not to cringe as she scrubbed at her black legs with our freshly laundered towels. It was deeply humbling and more than a little frustrating to acknowledge how my own pettiness could so easily overwhelm generosity, even as I enjoyed a breakthrough moment with Lotus.

That night as I read a bedtime story to Laini, she commented on how much better the apartment smelled. Giving me a side squeeze, my eight-year-old commented, "That probably wasn't easy, Mom. Good job." Then with a mischievous twinkle in her eye, she suggested, "You know, I'm not sure you had to go all in. You probably could have worn a swimsuit."

— • —

Despite some trying times, Lotus and I also shared deeply poignant moments together. One Saturday morning, she shyly asked me, "Auntie Emily, can you show me how to do makeup?" Laini looked up from her book, gave me an exaggerated wink, and quietly left the room. (Oh, how I have, and always will, appreciate my daughter's wise-beyond-her-years understanding!)

I excitedly invited Lotus to my bedroom, pulling out eyeliners, shadows, and lipsticks. As we faced the mirror together, I showed her how to accentuate her pretty eyes with liquid liner. She watched, wide-eyed, as I applied gloss to the center of her bow-shaped lips. Explaining what I was doing along the way, I commented, "Lotus, you look so pretty, and this is super fun. But you don't need makeup; you're beautiful just the way you are."

Then, catching me off guard, Lotus's face suddenly collapsed as she started to weep. For the first time in months, I witnessed this tough, prickly girl who pushed back and antagonized me on a regular basis totally breaking down. Placing a slender brush on the counter, I cupped her face in my hands and asked, "Lotus, what's wrong? I'm so sorry; I didn't mean to make you cry."

She hiccupped as she gradually regained control of her emotions. Red-eyed, she revealed: "Auntie Emily, no one has ever told me I'm beautiful. My mom said I'm ugly...too ugly to be a prostitute like her. She told me I'll never find work. And look at all the scars on my face from where she hurt me.... They make me look monstrous!"

As tears flowed silently down both our faces, Lotus took inventory of all her scars, recounting how she received each wound. Of all those terrible marks, I'll never forget the ones on the back of her left hand. She said, "I can't remember what I did to make her so angry. But my mom hooked her fingers into chicken claws and dug chunks of flesh out of my hand with the nail of her index finger. Once she made a hole here, she just kept digging. It was like she was trying to pull the bones right out of my hands!" I'll never forget Lotus's last comment as she stared reflectively at her hand: "Other kids at school have scabs and scars, too, but mine always look different."

Oomph. She had a way of doing that, of taking an ordinary conversation and catapulting it into something confoundingly tragic. But Lotus didn't even know she was doing it. Because all of it—the relatively ordinary moments and the extraordinarily terrible experiences—was all just a day in her life.

Later that week, we had a similar epiphany over dinner. On the weekends, our family ate together at the dining table. But

I had learned early on that our table topics were quite limited. I refrained from asking about friends; Lotus didn't have any friends at school, because the other moms wouldn't let their kids play with her. I avoided asking about classes; she struggled terribly, with her grades regularly ranking at the bottom of her class. Then, as I sought to think of an inoffensive topic, Lotus spoke up: "Auntie Emily, I need to find my father."

The temperature in the room felt as if it suddenly dropped ten degrees. We knew that Lotus's father was a well-known local gangster, an abusive pimp who had disappeared a few months back. After reportedly cheating at a local casino and disappearing with bags of stolen money, he had supposedly fled Shanghai. In all the time she'd lived with us, we had never heard her mention him.

I responded cautiously, "Why do you need to find your father? Is there something we can do for you instead?" Lotus vehemently shook her head: "No! I need *him*!" she insisted. "See, I lost my phone today and need to get a replacement SIM card, and I *must* get exactly the same mobile phone number, and my mobile number is connected to *his* national identification number, so I need *him* to help me get another SIM card." I adopted a reasonable tone of voice: "Lotus, I understand. But I think it's OK if you get a different phone number. We can buy a new one for you, and you won't have to go find your dad."

Lotus again shook her head, this time even more violently. "Auntie Emily, you don't understand. I need *my* phone number because my best friend only knows *that* number, and she's in hiding right now because her father murdered her mother last night and she has no other way to call me."

We all sat in stunned silence. Laini nudged me and quietly asked, "'*Bei mousha*' means 'murdered,' right?" I nodded and looked back at Lotus. "OK. I understand," I told her. "Tomorrow, let's go find him." Relief flooded her face, and as she shouted,

"Thank you!" she knocked over her bowl of soup, and then accidentally kicked the dog as she scrambled to grab a towel from the kitchen.

The weekend Lotus went looking for her dad was an inflection point for us. Instead of challenging me at every turn, instead of pushing for more, she took a protective stance toward our family. She started texting and calling people but never once revealed where she lived, or whom she was with. When she finally located her father, she found that he was staying just an hour's train ride away. With her familiarly defiant tone, she insisted on going to meet him alone.

All that afternoon and evening, we paced the hallway between the girls' rooms. We obsessively checked our phones in case we had received a text from her. We even ran out to the elevator lobby once, only to find our neighbor coming home from the store.

Finally, Lotus returned that evening, triumphantly holding her new cell phone tightly in hand. She exclaimed, "I got a new SIM card! My dad is so nice, he even bought me this smartphone! And guess what? My friend called! She's back in the countryside now, living with her mom's relatives because her dad's in jail. Good thing I got my old number, huh? Now you see why I had to have it, Auntie Emily?" Lotus prattled on and on.... I nearly forgot that her father was a dangerous man who sold women's bodies for a living.

That wasn't the last time I felt a strange mind meld with Lotus, when I could suddenly see the world through her eyes. When the outrageously unacceptable became normal, and abusive tyrants seemed kindly and sincere. Lotus volunteered at Sharon's youth center on the weekends and often returned to our apartment with stories from her old neighborhood. One day, she sadly shared that a timid nine-year-old boy, Xiao Qiang, had just been sent to the emergency room.

Xiao Qiang had needed his mom's signature, confirming agreement to an upcoming field trip to the Shanghai Urban Planning Exhibition Center in People's Square. Knowing his mom worked until four a.m. each day, the boy had been extremely anxious about bothering her. But the opportunity to go to People's Square was one he didn't want to miss! So, after school, he had returned home and knocked gently on his mom's door to ask for the signature.

The boy's mom yanked open her bedroom door and screeched, "What could possibly be so important that you feel the need to wake me right now?! You *know* I only have a few hours to sleep each day! You had better be bleeding, or I'll *make* you bleed!" Xiao Qiang had immediately taken two steps back, head lowered and hands raised in self-defense. "I'm sorry, Ma, I'm sorry. It's nothing. Go back to sleep." But it was already too late. She saw the paper, tore it out of his hand, and exploded in rage.

"You dare to wake me up, just so you can go have *fun*?! Do you know how hard I work just so you can go to school? Ingrate!" With a loud screech, she twisted the back of the boy's shirt tightly in her fist, and with all her pent-up fury, slammed him headfirst into her bureau.

The boy's skull cracked open like a watermelon. The mom panicked and rushed out of the apartment, wailing, "My boy fell down and he's hurt! Please help me!" Neighbors had heard the screaming through the paper-thin walls, and no one thought for a second that the boy had fallen. But together, they rushed him to the hospital.

Word spread quickly that Xiao Qiang had fallen into a coma. This was devastating because, in China, losing a few days at the critical age of nine can have big implications for a child's future. A couple of weeks are often enough for a student to start falling behind, impacting school grades and self-esteem. By the time the child takes the *Zhongkao* (middle test), which middle school-age kids take to earn a spot in high school, he or she may likely already be out of the running. Which leaves just one option: joining the throngs of fourteen-year-olds out working in the streets.

I found myself nodding as Lotus told us about the boy. I agreed it was sad that he was likely going to end up working in the streets and not going to high school.

It was a good half hour later when I stopped myself. "Wait a minute, this isn't *sad*. This is *unacceptable*!" I exclaimed. "A mother attacked her son. She cracked his head open!" Having been around so many similar stories, I found myself reacting only to the outcome for the child; seeing life through Lotus's eyes, I hadn't even been angered by the mother's actions. It was almost as if parents were expected to act this way, and all we could hope was for the children to make it through alive.

— · —

Months went by, and we settled into a relatively smooth rhythm with Lotus, who was now fifteen. On weekdays, she left so early in the morning to catch the bus, and arrived so late in the evening, that we were really together as a family only on the weekends. And then Lotus began heading out Saturday morning, not returning until late Sunday evening. When I asked her where she was staying, I received one vague reply after another. But after reviewing our options, my husband and I agreed that as long as she was continuing to improve at school and didn't bring home anything or anyone unsafe, we wouldn't overly parent the teenager.

The following weekend, we saw Lotus sneaking out the door, guiltily shrouding a big package with her jacket. I asked her, "Lotus, what are you taking out of the apartment? You're not in trouble; I'd just like to see what you're carrying, please."

In a heartbeat, I watched her round, frightened eyes narrow into angry slits. "It's not for me. And you said I could have as much food as I want. You're a *liar*! You're holding me here like a *prisoner*!" Her voice was shrill as she hurtled furious accusations at me.

This happened frequently. When Lotus was confronted with even the most innocent question, her emotions would quickly spiral from feeling defensiveness to feeling attacked and then unworthy...and unloved. We spent hours reassuring her that her place in our home was safe, no matter how she behaved or what questions we posed. On this particular Saturday morning, we reassured her that she was not a prisoner and slowly unpacked the bag that she had been holding so tightly. We found leftover cake from the previous evening's party, and handfuls of Halloween candy. I reassured Lotus, "You can absolutely have all of this...but it's not very healthy. Are you planning to eat it all yourself?"

Lotus again responded with outrage: "This crap? I don't even *like* sweets! This isn't for me at all!" Then she proceeded to tell us about Ting Ting.

Ting Ting was a ten-year-old girl who lived in the brothel where Lotus had been raised. But unlike Lotus's mother, Ting Ting's mother had never registered her children, which meant that both the girl and her five-year-old brother were "ghost children." Neither existed on paper, nor did they have the right to attend school. According to Lotus, the two children ran wild in the streets. She claimed the kids were left with no option but to steal food when hungry; they were often caught and beaten by shop clerks.

After hearing about how Lotus's friends were starving in the streets, our family began realizing how much food we wasted, and began regularly asking to have leftovers packed at restaurants. Our girl was an abrasive, volatile character, but she had a good heart and faithfully brought food packages to Ting Ting every weekend.

Then one day, Lotus asked, "Uncle Minki, you're such a good cook. Will you come to my neighborhood and cook Western food for the kids?"

That first trip, we brought salad and lasagna for fourteen kids, along with packs of construction paper and markers. Sharon had kindly agreed to open up her center for us to use. Most of the kids didn't enjoy the salad (the Chinese don't typically consume raw or cold vegetables), but they quickly gobbled up the lasagna.

That evening marked the first time we met Ting Ting. Right when we arrived, I noticed a quiet girl trailing me as I made my way in and out of the kitchen. Lotus burst into the small cooking area, shouting, "Ting Ting, get out of here! This is for us *adults* only." As Lotus categorically asserted her seniority, Laini and I exchanged secret smiles while we plated the food. It seemed that our spare room guest was equally bossy in and out of our home.

As the children ate that evening, we mingled with them. They were full of questions—and opinions. "This cheese...it's too *chewy*!" "The tomato sauce is too sour." "Cold, crispy vegetables...were you too lazy to cook them?" Wow, it was like a room full of tiny Lotuses. But the kids were also curious and charming.

Skinny little Ting Ting looked my daughter up and down and asked me, "Does she get to eat like this a lot?" When I answered in the affirmative, she followed with, "How many times a day does she get to eat?" When Ting Ting heard we ate full meals three times a day, her eyes bugged out. "*Wa! Three times a day!*" she exclaimed. "No wonder you're all so fat." That feeling of guilty gluttony for having access to three full meals a day stays with me to this day.

As does the memory of the cutest little five-year-old boy. The spunky little guy waddled up to me and tugged on my shirt, saying, "Auntie, in America, is it true that kids get a special day all for themselves, to wear shiny hats and eat cake?" I thought for a moment and exclaimed, "Yes! I think you're talking about birthdays. That is when we celebrate the day we were born." I didn't know whether to laugh or cry when that little guy suddenly leapt into the air. "I can't believe it!" he shouted. "A whole day just for one kid. Shiny hat and creamy cake. Wow! I want to go to America."

I playfully brushed his hair out of his eyes and said, "Well, we celebrate birthdays here in China, too. When's *your* birthday?" The hyperactive little boy stilled. He scrunched up his face and pulled at the frayed collar of his yellow shirt. "I don't know," he answered. "How do you know when your birthday is?" He then raised his voice, "Hey, kids! Do you know when your birthday is?"

In amazement, I sought to keep up with the ensuing chaos. Some kids knew their birthdays. Many didn't. Those who did mocked those who didn't. Those who didn't immediately put up their fists, ready for battle, their faces red and sweaty. But after living with Lotus all those months, I had learned to manage quickly escalating emotions, and clapped my hands for attention.

"Hey, kids! I want you to listen to me! Did Auntie Emily and Uncle Minki bring you Western food to try today?"

They chorused, "Yes!"

"Would you like us to bring you a birthday cake next time?"

They thundered in unison, "Yes!"

Then the room grew quiet as they peered at me expectantly. I took advantage of my moment, and inspiration struck: "How about we come back every month and throw a birthday party? If you know your birthday, you can write it down on this red piece of paper. If you don't, you get to pick a date for your birthday and put it on the same paper, OK?"

A cacophony of questions burbled feverishly around the room. "I'll answer all your questions," I called out. "But you need to be orderly and raise your hands, please. Now, one at a time!"

"Will everybody get cake, or just the birthday kids?"

"Will you bring us presents?"

"Can I have a birthday *every* month?"

I answered questions for the next thirty minutes, roughly sketching out a plan as we went. My wonderful husband stood in the back of the room, nodding and giving me a thumbs-up. My daughter recorded the entire exchange on an iPhone, her expression alternating between bemusement and pride.

By the end of the evening, we had agreed to come back each month with dinner, birthday cake, and presents for everyone. But only the birthday kids would get to wear the shiny conical hats. The kids were fabulously excited! Later, as our family packed up and wiped down the kitchen, we looked dazedly at one another.... What had I just gotten us into?

That evening, Lotus paid her one and only compliment to me ever: "Auntie Emily, you're not so bad." Smiling, I asked her to continue coming with us to manage all the kids. "Of course! You silly Westerners could never handle those kids without me," she scornfully replied.

We may have overdone it on the first birthday party. Recruiting six friends to come with us, including some of my Starbucks team, we planned to bring dinner, cake, party decorations, and party favors for twenty kids. But everyone was so excited to throw the party, we ended up with three meals, two cakes, and boxes of favors.

The kids loved it! While the constant clamor and endless bickering left us exhausted, the evening was undoubtedly a great success. Then, over the next few months, we hit our stride as an informal little team. And delightfully, our friendships grew in depth—with our own friends, and also with Lotus. We learned that nothing cultivates a meaningful friendship like new experiences in unknown territory with others, side by side.

Also, the kids began to settle down. At first, they argued over the first serving or the biggest slice of cake. But soon, the bickering was replaced by patience and small kindnesses. A collateral benefit: my introspective daughter was pulled out of her reserved state by those raucous and fun-loving kids. As much as sharing life with Lotus pulled me out of my comfort zone, those birthday parties pulled Laini out of hers. Going in, she saw herself as one of us, but the kids saw her as one of them. Before long, she was sitting with the kids at the table, and I often found her conversing with Ting Ting.

— • —

As the children in Lotus's neighborhood matured, so did she. With Sharon's help, Ting Ting and her brother were soon able to secure the paperwork to begin attending school on one side of town. On the other side, living with us, Lotus completely transformed her grades. Through painstaking effort and sheer will, the fifteen-year-old earned a coveted spot at a vocational high school. Soon, she moved out of our apartment to board at the educational institution. She was the first in her family to achieve a higher-level education, and we gladly listened as she boasted about being *di yi ming*, the highest-ranked student in mathematics. She also complained loudly about her room-mates and the cramped quarters; six girls shared a room the size of a large closet, with triple bunk beds on either side of the room: "They're so *dirty*! They don't even shower every day, and I'm the only one who sweeps the floor. Do you know what they call me? They call me 'The Cleaner!'"

At this, our whole family burst out laughing...my, how far Lotus had come! Shortly after our last dinner with Lotus, we relocated to the States after eight years in Shanghai. We left, content in the knowledge that Lotus was thriving in her vocational school, and proud of all she was accomplishing.

Now, one year later, our friends continue to faithfully host the monthly birthday parties. The children continue to blossom and, like Lotus, seem to breathe easier in the newly planted beliefs that they are smart, able, and worthy.

Living with Lotus, we witnessed incredible miracles of self-discovery, growth, and triumph. We realized that many people simply can't imagine a different future if they aren't afforded an opportunity to see what's possible. And when we help expand their worldview, we have the opportunity to plant seeds of dreams that can never again be ignored or forgotten. Even when it feels incredibly uncomfortable or difficult, being willing to journey outside our comfort zone is overwhelmingly rewarding. And it is our social legacy, the knowledge of our Offense and our Offer, that gives us courage to brave the unpaved road.

The Creatures
Kramatorsk, Ukraine, 2005

"This is simply not possible!" the orphanage Director barked with disbelief, as he flipped through the photos in his hand.

Amanda beamed with pride as she caught glimpses of her two beautiful boys in each print. Over three years ago, she and her husband had adopted their boys—then two years old—from this same Ukrainian orphanage. The children had both been born with cerebral palsy, and at the time Amanda met them, they were significantly malnourished, weighing just fourteen pounds each. Though they hadn't even been able to lift their heads when she adopted them, the photos now revealed her smiling boys engaged in ordinary activities like sitting at the dinner table and playing in the park.

"In America, we treat special-needs children just like regular kids. We believe they have the ability to learn, so we provide them with therapy that helps them live happy, productive lives," she explained enthusiastically.

Shaking his head in wonder, Antoli, the orphanage director, lifted his head to gaze at Amanda. "Can you teach us?" he asked.

— • —

Amanda's mind immediately jumped to the beautiful blond therapist, Kym, who had treated her boys. Kym had just opened her new practice in Arkansas when Amanda began bringing the boys, Dimitri and Aleksei, to weekly treatments. The adoptive mom had been delighted to see such dramatic improvements in both boys in just a few months' time. So, after she had returned from Ukraine and as that week's session was drawing to a close, Amanda hesitatingly asked, "Kym, do you have a few extra minutes?"

Watching the boys play on a nearby mat, Amanda recounted her recent discussion with the orphanage director. Her boys had been among the first two special-needs children adopted from the home Antoli ran, because potential parents were normally steered to the healthier babies. Yet, after witnessing her boys' improvement, the new mom believed that with basic treatment, more special-needs orphans could be deemed adoptable. She asked if Kym might have textbooks or brochures they could send to Ukraine. Half an hour later, Amanda's face broke into a huge grin when Kym exclaimed, "Why don't we just go there and show them?"

Having recently opened the clinic, Kym realized she was taking a risk, leaving for ten days to volunteer her services in an unfamiliar foreign country. Yet she felt confident in what she had to offer and, as she perused the printed material available, was certain that going in person would be more effective. Most instructional therapy guides had been designed for professionals and would be difficult to understand, even if translated. Furthermore, one of her new employees, an enthusiastic therapist named Karen, had also volunteered to join her on the trip.

—·—

"You know how this is going to end, Karen," intoned the therapist's husband, John Michael. "You can't even go to a dog shelter without crying! How are you going to visit an orphanage in Ukraine?"

"They're *asking* to learn more, babe!" Karen responded. "This is our chance to help so many little orphan babies get adopted. How could we possibly say no?" Her eyes shone with fervor and determination as she grasped her husband's muscled arm. "Anyway, it's just a ten-day trip. Who knows what will happen? We'll see how much we can do in that short period of time."

Despite his anxiety, John Michael supported her ambitions, going online in the evenings to learn about Ukrainian culture. He smiled to himself as he listened to Karen's evening phone calls with Kym.

"What's the weather like over there?"

"I don't know.... What's the currency over there?"

"No idea.... Do you think we should pack amenities, or will the hotel provide them?"

"OK, we clearly don't know what to prepare for *ourselves*, but we *do* know what the kids need. Let's focus on that first!"

Karen and Kym spent the next few weeks printing out instructions for simple physical therapy exercises. They often called Amanda to learn about the orphanage and were shocked to learn there were no toys in the building at all. The ladies enthusiastically bought and collected simple non-battery toys, like handheld rattles. They bought lengths of PVC pipes to make mobiles that could hang over cribs, to help with important sensory development.

Finally, the morning of their long-awaited trip arrived. Karen and Kym met at the airport and immediately burst into laughter. Preparing to head out on their adventure, the two therapists struggled toward each other, each stooped under the weight of an overstuffed backpack and dragging two enormous suitcases behind her. Each woman had packed only one backpack for herself; the four suitcases were filled entirely with things for the orphans. As they met Amanda and boarded the airplane together, Kym declared, "This is going to be the trip of a lifetime!" If only she had known that this was just the beginning.

— • —

"Before we go, I must prepare you for a few things," said the smartly dressed interpreter, Olga. In Ukraine, the young lady had already helped many international families with their adoptions over the years. She provided not only language services but also an important cultural bridge for those entering Ukraine for the first time. Now, she would be joining Amanda and the therapists on their visit to the orphanage, to help translate the upcoming training sessions.

"We care for orphans differently here in Ukraine. This orphanage houses 156 children. And for those with special needs, the caretakers do their best to keep the children healthy. But they are understaffed and not always well trained. You must not judge them," Olga stated firmly.

The interpreter continued in the same unflinching voice, "You must not cry. Hold back all your emotions. Any reaction will be seen as extreme rudeness. The caretakers will become very offended, and you may be asked to leave."

Karen and Kym exchanged nervous glances. In preparing for the trip, the two women had already shed tears as they hand-crafted therapy equipment, just thinking about so many babies lying alone, without a toy to cuddle or a mobile hanging above to occupy their attention.

Standing up a little straighter, Kym said calmly, "We understand. We will do everything we can to demonstrate respect to the caretakers and the local culture. We just want to help those little babies. We're ready."

— · —

An hour later, the Americans entered the orphanage with small, uncertain steps. Their wide eyes swept the room, taking in the austere setting as they plastered big, close-lipped smiles on their faces. Directed to the main playroom, where prospective parents met the orphans, Kym was relieved to at least observe a few therapy mats scattered on the floor. She took a seat at one end of the large room and prepared to begin her first round of assessments. Clipboard in hand, Karen sat beside her, glancing down at her notes and mentally bracing herself for what she had come here to do. Yet, despite Karen's having planned for this moment over the previous two months, her eyes widened in surprise as she looked up. She took in the long, orderly line of children, the littlest ones carried by caretakers, in front of her makeshift desk. Glancing at her watch, Karen realized they could afford only three minutes per child if they were going to get through all the kids in the allotted time.

Those adorable little faces began to blur in front of her as the same routine was repeated countless times. A child was plopped down on the desk in front of the therapists. Running through the exercises as quickly as she could, Kym made her assessment while Karen hastily jotted notes for each little one. As she flipped to a fresh piece of paper, the next child was already seated in front of them, silently staring at them with unblinking eyes.

As she completed her fifth assessment, Karen was suddenly able to put her finger on the source of her unease. From the moment they had stepped foot into the orphanage, despite the fact that the old building housed hundreds of children, the place was eerily quiet. She had heard no crying, no laughter, no pitter-patter of little feet.

Now, as the little ones waited in an endless line in front of her, the therapists contemplated the same solemn stillness. The toddlers stood in what looked like a freeze frame, staring vacantly ahead or looking down at the floor. They didn't fidget or engage with one another at all. They simply stood in a tomb-like silence...waiting. Rubbing the goosebumps from her arms, Karen flipped the page and cheerfully called out, "Next?"

"This is Ivan Vitaliyovych Likholetov. Two years old. Brain problem." The tiny boy peered curiously at Karen. Red hair stood up in tufts all over his head, and his eyes crossed adorably over a small, endearing smile.

Karen looked up. "What a big name for such a tiny little guy," she thought, her eyes sparkling. As her heart flip-flopped with a combination of enchantment and reluctance to let him go, the therapist forced herself to finish recording his notes. By the time she looked back up, Ivan had been whisked away and a little girl sat in his place.

Many hours later, as the therapists settled back into their hotel room, Karen exclaimed, "That was the longest day of my life!" She flexed and unflexed her cramped fingers as Kym cracked her own back with a painful grimace. Anticipating the long night that still lay ahead of them, the friends took time for a warm meal and compared reactions from the day. The curative effect of finally releasing their pent-up emotions soon left both women in tears.

"Why was it so silent? It was eerie how so many children could be so completely still!"

"I know! What about the fact that they had zero toys? Those kids just lie in their cots, staring at the ceiling all day."

"Did you see...Ivan?" Karen then asked, hesitatingly.

Kym's eyes shot up from her shish kebab. "Uh-oh, I know that voice, Karen. You do remember what John Michael said," she said, the note of warning in her voice overshadowed by affectionate warmth.

"I know, I know," Karen hastily replied. "He was just *so cute*! Anyway, we have a whole night of work ahead of us. Let's get to it."

The friends sat side by side on their hotel beds, chugging bottled water and lukewarm Nescafé instant coffee well into the morning hours. By daybreak, the therapists had created one packet for every child who had passed through their hands, listing assessments and simple exercises, all painstakingly handwritten on sheets of notebook paper. Little tips were penned in the margins, like "Please make eye contact with each child! This will improve sensory integration," and "A piece of fabric held between two adults makes a wonderful swing."

The next morning, hugging armloads of paper, Karen and Kym returned to the orphanage. This time the main room was filled to overflowing, as caregivers from other orphanages joined to watch and learn.

Each child was once again placed in front of the therapists, as caregivers listened attentively to the personalized recommendations. Olga translated the instructions, simultaneously jotting notes in Russian for future reference. As the crowd of children slowly thinned, Ivan eventually made his way to the front of the line. Once again, Karen felt her heart leap painfully as she laid eyes on that lopsided little smile. She gave him an extra squeeze before passing him back into the human chain of tiny bodies.

— • —

Despite facing a seemingly endless series of challenges, Karen and Kym felt like they were getting the hang of the orphanage after a couple of days there. It appeared the orphanage director had also decided to trust them, because on their last day, Antoli invited the therapists upstairs. Looking at him quizzically, Kym commented, "I didn't realize there were rooms up here. Why haven't we seen these children yet?"

Then the therapists, Amanda, and Antoli stepped into the Group Four room.

Kym's attention was immediately drawn to a little girl with big brown eyes. Unlike most of the twenty-five babies in the room, she had stirred when the women entered, shifting her small, skeletal body to try to gaze at the visitors. "Why is that baby's ankle tied to the bedpost?" Kym asked, doing her best to keep her voice even.

Olga translated Antoli's answer: "She keeps trying to stand up, and that makes the caregivers' job more difficult. You see, there are only two women who care for this entire room."

Kym nodded slowly as she approached the tiny girl with large eyes and curly hair. Just as Amanda had whispered to her boys years ago, the therapist now quietly said, "You're coming home with me, little one."

Kym quickly convinced the director to allow them to help with Group Four, just as she and Karen had done with the children downstairs. The two therapists spent time with each of the children deemed "unadoptable" in that upstairs room, preparing treatment documents for each one. And that's how the ladies closed out their last day at the orphanage. The next day, they would visit the Institution for Mentally and Physically Disabled

Orphans, an ominous building where special-needs orphans were transferred at age four if they hadn't been adopted.

The next morning, Olga repeated the now familiar words: "Before we go, I must prepare you for a few things. The institution houses 325 children, so resources are stretched even thinner. There has never been an adoption from the institute, and over 80 percent of children die within their first six months. You will not expect the same hope, or the same interest, to help the children physically improve. You must remember, these children are already four years old."

Karen maintained her steadfast silence but acerbically thought, "Oh, yeah. They're practically ready to enter the workforce."

Olga continued, "Because the orphanage director was so impressed with the training you provided, we have special permission for you to visit the institution. But please be aware, you are the first Americans to ever set foot inside. You will treat this privilege with the respect it deserves."

An hour later as the group stepped foot out of the car and took in the monstrous gray building looming before them, Karen couldn't help but feel like she was walking into a horror movie. Goosebumps pricked up and down her arms as they entered the institution, the now familiar eerie hush of silent children descending on the visitors like a bleak, weighty fog.

— · —

While malnourishment and delayed development in the orphanage had disturbed the therapists, they had known the caregivers were doing the best they could. Here at the institution, a whole new level of horror greeted them.

As Olga and the Americans entered the first room, they gazed upon twenty-five cots, each occupied by an infant-sized body. Every child's stomach was distended by malnutrition, and their feet were swollen and tinged with blue from lack of movement. A tiny girl with Down syndrome lay in a pool of her own vomit, painfully aspirating some of the liquid. A little boy with spina bifida lolled on his cot, loops of his intestines lying beside his body on the filthy pallet. "This is nothing but slow euthanasia," Amanda whispered in horror.

A nearly hysterical Kym ran out of the room, one hand clamped over her mouth. It wasn't that the little boy had spina bifida; she had treated the birth defect before. It wasn't that his internal organs were lying exposed or the putrid stench of infection. Rather, it was the utterly blank expression in the small boy's eyes. He was just moments away from dying a horrendous death. Overwhelmed by the scene in front of her, the therapist had hurriedly raced outside to be sick.

"Oh, she's just got a sensitive stomach," Karen commented lightly to the stern-looking director of the institution. "I'm sure she'll be back in a minute; happens all the time."

A few moments later, as Kym splashed water on her face in the washroom, Karen and Amanda continued to make their way across the next room. Their heartache only deepened as they took in the endless rows of beds, each metal structure stoically bearing one skinny, unmoving body. Walking slowly across the room, Karen did her best to maintain a neutral expression as she took in the scores of listless children. Silently ticking off unmistakable symptoms of malnutrition, she paused to gently touch one girl who was covered in scabies. The tenderhearted therapist suppressed a gasp as the child's limp arm dropped leadenly into her hand. The appendage was implausibly emaciated, the skin nearly translucent despite the heavy smattering of ugly scabs and blisters that covered it.

Karen looked down with dismay, realizing the girl's threadbare bedsheets was soaked in urine. In fact, the bedding around her head was also drenched. Horrified, Karen made a mental note to ask about the cloudy fluid that had puddled around the child's neck and shoulders.

At that moment, the institute's director brusquely muttered something at the visitors. Olga quickly translated, "He wants to know when you will begin. I suggest we commence immediately," she added nervously, glancing at the man's impatient expression.

At that exact moment, Kym rushed in to rejoin the group and chirped with false cheer, "Fantastic! Where can we set up?"

Quickly, the therapists realized that the institution would not allow the same setup that had worked so well at the orphanage. The director laughed derisively as Olga translated their suggestions, replying, "We shall not move the creatures. We do not have the time or resource. If you want to assess them, you can walk from one creature to the next."

Even as the friends sought to curtail any emotional reaction, their fingers found each other's behind the manila folders Karen gripped tightly in one hand. They squeezed each other fiercely as they listened to the director of the institution refer to the children as "creatures."

The stern man continued, "You may assess each one. You will not address them or, in fact, speak at all. If a creature becomes disruptive, it will be removed."

— . —

Hours later, having methodically worked their way up and down the rows of grimy cots, the therapists gathered up their things. Olga agreed with the director on a time for them to return and share their assessment of each child. Shakily, Karen took a deep breath and stood up to go.

Following her friend, she stumbled blindly into her friend's back when Kym drew to an abrupt halt. A tiny gasp escaped her lips as the visitors struggled to absorb the scene unfolding before them. Stern-faced caretakers were scattered around the room, each slowly pushing a squeaky metal cart ferrying a large pot of broth. As each adult paused briefly beside the next child, she sloppily scooped a ladle of the broth, trailing large, greasy drops from the pot to the youngster. The ladle was then unceremoniously upturned over an open, waiting mouth. Each body lay completely still, arms stiff and straight against the cot, as broth splashed all over each little face. Frantic gulping, coughing, and occasional choking sounds were the only noises that echoed in the large, barren room.

Karen now understood how the scabies-covered girl had come to lie on a soaking-wet cot. The young therapist forced her eyes to the floor, quickened her pace, and exited the room as quickly as she could. She sensed that she wasn't the only one about to completely lose it. After saying hasty goodbyes and pulling away from the morbid scene, the three Americans pulled to the side of the road and allowed the car to idle. Karen's body shook with agonized sobs as she forlornly thought of little Ivan. There was no way she was going to let him end up in that institution.

— • —

The therapists returned to the institute two days later to deliver their recommendations, with Amanda once again joining them. Kym was normally cheerful and optimistic, but after their experience, the astute clinic owner wondered how readily those working at the institution would accept their opinions. And before she could even complete her first assessment, Olga was forced to translate the defiant objections of one gray-haired caretaker who had spent most of her life working in the institution. The matronly veteran snorted bitterly, "You expect us to have time to do these things? We are already busy feeding and changing them. Every day we must also bury the dead ones and sweep the sidewalks!"

Another caretaker challenged the women, "Are you really doctors from America? I demand to see your paperwork!" After scrutinizing their credentials, the woman finally shook the sheaf of papers triumphantly. "Aha! You see, I knew it. You are here to treat *children*, not *orphans*."

As Olga translated, Amanda took in Kym's puzzled expression and jumped in. She spoke quickly and quietly, hiding her distaste: "To Ukrainians, orphans are not children. They are something less than human and live with the same stigma into adulthood, if they are lucky enough to survive the orphanage. This is why the director refers to them as 'creatures.'"

The next day, the ladies packed their bags and returned to the States. The word "creature" seemed to echo in their minds as ghostly visages of orphans visited them in their dreams. Even before they landed back at home, the informal team had already agreed to return to Antoli's orphanage a few months later. In fact, unbeknownst to them, that first trip had opened the door to the three women's social legacy.

Amanda, Kym, and Karen returned to Ukraine five more times over the next few years, helping hundreds of orphans overcome physical challenges and connect with forever families. Little cross-eyed Ivan Vitaliyovych Likholetov is now known as Lance Ivan Hairston. Inspired by Amanda's joy in mothering her delightful boys, Dimitri and Aleksei ("Dima" and "Leks"), Karen had returned to Ukraine with her husband to bring the cute cross-eyed boy home. And in the next few years, as Lance absorbed good nutrition and loving care, the boy who had been born with cerebral palsy and autism soon learned to feed himself and to walk unassisted. Today, he is a high school sophomore who loves dancing to country music, and nothing gives him more joy than the adrenaline rush of riding a jet ski.

Like Karen, Kym also returned to Ukraine within a year from their first trip, to bring that little curly-haired girl from Group Four home, just before she was going to be shipped to the institution. Having lived her entire life in the upper-level Group Four room tied to a bedpost, the four-year-old, Myrah, weighed just eighteen pounds. She had never left the orphanage and had never used a toilet, but rather had lain on a wet, stinking cloth diaper until it was changed once every other day. Kym will never forget the day little Myrah first felt the wind. "All those things we grow up with and take for granted, like the natural elements, were completely new to her. She'd been raised in a windowless room, only exposed to artificial light and completely unaware of the outdoors. As a mild breeze blew that first day outside, she opened her little mouth and shook so hard, I thought she was having a seizure. But she was just excited! To this day, Myrah loves being outside, soaking in the sunlight or getting drenched in the rain. I don't think she'll ever have enough."

Amanda later adopted a third Ukrainian child, this time a girl. Having caught sight of the girl years earlier when she had first adopted her boys, she had relentlessly pursued the adoption. Like Kym, she finalized the paperwork just days before the four-year-old girl, Elena, was going to be shipped to the institution.

Though Amanda had adopted children from Antoli's orphanage before, this time was different. Early in the process, Elena was made aware that the adoption was in progress, so every time the Americans visited, she cheerfully greeted them with "Hooray, my mother is here! Come, Mom, you sleep here with me."

Then, three and a half years after bringing her boys home, Amanda relaxed, amused in the back seat of a taxi as the little girl in her lap cried, "Please don't stop! Just go, go!" every time the car paused at an intersection. That same evening as the two snuggled on a bunk on the dark train for their overnight journey, Amanda slowly turned her head to see if Elena had fallen asleep. She could only burst out laughing when she was met with Elena's wide, joyful eyes fixed on her mother's face and a huge, glowing smile stretched from ear to ear. Just this year, Elena ("Lena"), an avid Arkansas Razorbacks fan and an artist who loves to read, sing, and tell jokes, graduated from high school.

Today in Antoli's orphanage, there is no more Group Four in the upstairs room. All the children have been integrated into the lower level, and all are deemed adoptable. TEAMworks, the nonprofit leg of Kym's clinic, has also expanded beyond Ukraine to South America and Asia. All because one woman, then two more, and now sixteen families in Northwest Arkansas have been willing to step out onto the unpaved road. As a result of their courage, the lives of Lance, Myrah, Dima, Leks, Lena, and hundreds of orphans' lives have been forever changed.

The Last House
Georgia, 2012

"Our community simply *must* do something for them," Linda's strident voice urged over the phone. "Their two-year-old was just killed in a mall fire last week, and they're on their way back to Atlanta now."

Kitti's hand gripped her mobile phone tightly as she digested the shocking news. The frizzy-haired toddler had lived with her parents just across the complex. And a few short weeks ago, they had flown to Qatar to visit family. She took a deep, shaky breath before responding, "The baby *died*? They must be devastated! What happened out there?"

Linda numbly shared what she knew. "The Villaggio Mall in Doha is incredibly luxe, but it seems the daycare was unlicensed.

They hadn't built to code, and the emergency exit was locked from the outside." She paused before continuing in a muted voice, "Kitti, the babies and their teachers were trapped inside when the fire began. All thirteen toddlers were killed."

With a heavy heart, Kitti hung up the phone a few minutes later, agreeing to meet her friend for lunch. She shook her head sadly at the unexpected tragedy. At least she had her work cut out for her. She and Linda would rally the community to come together and support the devastated couple. Pausing in her thoughts, Kitti tilted her head and allowed herself a small smile as she appreciated how different her life was today, compared to just a few years prior.

Raised in conservative Nashville, Tennessee, Kitti had lived most of her adult life in the predominantly white suburbs of Atlanta. Now she found herself collaborating with Linda, her lesbian neighbor, to organize community support for a young couple who had lost their daughter in the Middle East.

— • —

Three years prior, Kitti and Bill Murray had upended their life when they decided to sell their home. With the last of their four sons headed off to college, the empty nesters had agreed to exchange their large, comfortable house for a two-bedroom apartment downtown. Of course, leaving their cozy cul-de-sac in the suburbs wasn't easy, but Bill had accepted a role as Area Director for an exciting company called Apartment Life. Responsible for boosting resident retention and building a sense of community in a particular building, he and Kitti moved into the building themselves as he began his new job.

And not long after making the transition, Kitti experienced a major epiphany. "As an individual and as a couple, I'd never felt we had an 'us versus them' mentality, but once we moved into this complex that housed such diverse people from all walks of life, we realized that we'd burst out of a bubble we hadn't even known we'd lived in!" And once outside that bubble, she exulted like an unleashed puppy, bounding joyfully from one new friend to another.

Apartment Life ended up being the dream job for the couple. Quiet, steady Bill found himself positioned to apply all his people skills as he helped incoming residents move in and connect with their neighbors. Meanwhile, his beautiful, extroverted wife organized pancake breakfasts, book clubs, and pool parties for the community.

In fact, Kitti had first met Linda at one of the summer's community breakfasts, when Linda had surprised everyone with her exceptional culinary skills. As the impromptu chef casually whipped up a delicious hollandaise sauce, her bohemian partner Molly stood beside her, oversized red glasses perched atop her head as she plated eggs Benedict for the quickly forming line of eager neighbors. The two lively, witty ladies had effortlessly transformed a polite community breakfast into a delightful feast among friends.

That evening, as Kitti and Bill took their evening stroll, they waved a friendly hello to Linda and Molly, who were seated comfortably on their porch enjoying the quiet evening. The women waved back, and soon the two couples were sharing a bottle of wine and chatting like they'd known one another all their lives.

Hours later, after exchanging hugs and promises to return the favor soon, the Murrays headed back to their apartment. Strolling arm in arm under the starlit sky, the couple marveled at how completely opposite they were from the ladies. From politics to religion, geography to careers, they couldn't have sat on more opposing ends of every spectrum. Yet, because of the apartment community, the four diverse adults had become fast friends.

Life continued to expand as Kitti and Bill lavished care on their neighbors and connected with more individuals. They felt real momentum as the neighborhood came together around a memorial for the little girl who had been lost to that tragic mall fire in Qatar. And Kitty's book club soon expanded to the point where she realized they'd never choose a book that everyone would appreciate! So instead, the varied residents wrote their own rules, each bringing a book they'd read that week and sharing it with the others. Before long, neighbors were exposed to new authors and genres, and the get-togethers began to stretch languidly across each Sunday afternoon. Eventually, sturdy mugs of hot coffee were traded for twinkling glasses of wine as stimulating discussions continued into the twilight hours. And always, Kitti could be found seated comfortably in the middle of the group, legs tucked under her on the couch and her short, signature ash-blond hair swept elegantly to one side.

Then, after three fulfilling years of apartment living, Kitti and Bill began to revisit conversations about "the last house." For years, they had dreamt about their final home. A large kitchen for Kitti, who loved to feed masses of hungry people. A spacious library for Bill's extensive book collection. In their conversations, the last house had come to represent the crowning chapter of their lives, a place where they would host groups of friends and provide a second home for their nine grandchildren. While the house retained a similar shape in their imaginations, the setting for it had unexpectedly evolved in the previous couple of years.

Now, Kitti couldn't imagine returning to the relaxed suburbs of their earlier days. The vivacious people connector had grown to love the adventure of living with so many fascinating humans from such varied backgrounds. Both Kitti and Bill loved living amidst this rich tapestry of cultures and languages.

But where should they settle? Their complex in the city was wonderful, yet the two-bedroom apartment had become too small to host their growing number of grandchildren on the weekends. Scrolling through articles on his phone one Saturday morning, Bill asked, "Hey, did you realize the most diverse square mile in America is just thirty minutes northeast of downtown Atlanta?" As they enjoyed their morning coffee, he and Kitti researched the city of Clarkston together, learning that 43 percent of residents were foreign-born, and that nearly sixty nationalities were represented in the small 1.4-square-mile town.[1] Because of its access to public transportation and affordable housing, the majority of which were rental units, the government had identified Clarkston as a good landing place for displaced people. "Let's take a drive down there this weekend!" Kitty proposed excitedly.

The next day, the Murrays drove across the small town, wide-eyed as they took in the unexpected diversity coexisting side by side: a Vietnamese Buddhist temple, the Balageru Food Mart, a Methodist church, and Numsok Oriental Market. Other retail outlets posted signs only in Amharic or Nepali script. They watched as Asian women garbed in traditional silk *qipao* waved across the street at women in bright African headscarves.

"Well, this is it!" Kitti declared triumphantly, as Bill turned the car around and began driving home. "This is where we'll build the last house!"

For the last few years, the couple had loved nurturing the diverse community in their apartment complex. Now, serving a refugee community seemed like the logical next step. With her natural gift of hospitality and charismatic personality that drew others like a magnet, Kitti could become family for those who sought community far from their homes. As the pieces clicked into place, Kitti glimpsed their future down an unpaved road and exclaimed to her husband, "This is what we were *made* to do!"

Kitti soon became acquainted with the residents of Clarkston, sampling the delicious flavors and unique customs of more ethnic groups than she could count. And as she shared snacks and tea with people from Burma, Iraq, Eritrea, Somalia, Afghanistan, and Congo, the woman from the suburbs listened intently to devastating stories of war, violence, and unimaginable hardship. Hearing those stories of torture in Syria, religious persecution in Bhutan, and families torn apart in Vietnam and Burundi often left her sobbing and embracing her new friends. Kitti felt charged with determination to help them build fulfilling new lives in America.

Soon, the grandmother of nine children began to nurture the seeds of a new dream. She envisioned a coffee shop that would become a space where refugee neighbors could rest, meet, and work. Instead of Kitti's slowly building relationships and introducing one neighbor to another over time, this space could serve as an extension of her living room where everyone was welcome.

Furthermore, the refugees who made up over a third of Clarkston's population[2] wouldn't just be beneficiaries of the store. Kitti envisioned training the immigrants to give them skills, so that they could introduce their own countries' coffee rituals and take an active part in welcoming people to the neighborhood.

A few weeks after moving to Clarkston, Kitti and a few neighbors hosted a community block party to embrace the summer season. Bringing people together as she always did, Kitti thought the opportunity might help her gauge interest in her coffee shop concept. Standing nervously outside, not knowing what to expect, she began to second-guess herself. Was the need she had perceived really there? As she was a newcomer to the area, would the neighborhood appreciate her efforts? Yet soon, Kitti was smiling broadly as her twinkling blue eyes took in the eighty people who streamed in for her event.

Confirming there was enthusiastic interest for a neighborhood artisanal coffee shop, Kitti next realized her biggest challenge would be in creating a welcoming space that also told a more gracious and accurate refugee story. The best way to do this, she felt, was to hire displaced people who could become the heart of the coffee shop, representing that complex story with who they were as people and how they did their work every day.

First, Kitti raised funds to purchase a used truck and rent some open space in front of a car dealership. She consulted friends and experts on what it would take to operate the business, Refuge Coffee. Then she opened the coffee truck in the parking lot, powered by a diesel generator, with just one full-time and one part-time employee. Eventually, Refuge Coffee expanded to multiple locations. With each new site, more refugees were trained and employed.

Having designed Refuge Coffee as an extension of her own last house, nothing gave Kitti more pleasure than immersing herself in the camaraderie of her team during their morning "family meetings." Latte-complexioned employees from Afghanistan, Nepal, and Syria sat alongside mocha-skinned team members from Eritrea and Ethiopia, who leaned against the ebony bodies of their Congolese friends.

Displaced people who had escaped terrors no human should ever have to live through slowly began to heal from years of trauma. Learning and working alongside other baristas from enemy countries, the team members also learned to cast aside cultural barriers. And through every step of their journey, Kitti and Bill walked steadfastly alongside their team.

— · —

Leon Shombana was the very first trainee at Refuge Coffee, a former high school teacher from the Democratic Republic of

Congo. When Kitti first met the tall, muscular man, he was driving three hours a day to labor at a chicken processing plant. Then, as the Congolese man joined Refuge Coffee, his amazing work ethic and gentle kindness helped bring their concept to life in a soulful, human way. Yet, despite the man's warm disposition, the woman who had raised four boys sensed a deep sadness beneath his big, hearty smile. She soon discovered that he'd left four children behind in Congo. In fact, his story was all too familiar in the small city of Clarkston.

With his thick eyebrows framing wise eyes and a strong face, Leon recounted how his home had been attacked, and his father shot and killed. When everyone fled the violence, his wife and children also ran, while he was away at work. And in the pandemonium that followed, Leon lost track of his family. But now, after eight years with Refuge Coffee, the man has found a new home and support network. Growing with the company and emotionally bolstered by Kitti and the team, Leon has managed to find three of his children. And just last year, he stood alongside the entire staff as they tearfully greeted his two sons, Archange and Christophe, when they arrived in America to live with their father.

Over time, Refuge Coffee has come to serve as an unofficial town center, and Kitti's team members have grown with one another, becoming a tight-knit family. Kitti has shared countless coffees and tears with each member of her staff. She mourned with a young girl named Ndoole when she heard of how the girl had hidden for hours under her dead brother's corpse, even as she watched her other three brothers escape their burning village. Kitti stood by twenty-two-year-old Somaya, who struggled to provide as the primary breadwinner for her entire family back in Iran. Recently, as the "American parents" of Ahmad from Damascus, she and Bill threw a rehearsal dinner for him and his new American fiancée. And the whole Refuge Coffee team has rallied to help Frey set up her first business, selling rich Ethiopian tapestries and paying fair wages to women back home for their meticulous handicraft.

Kitti has successfully realized her dream, setting up an artisanal coffee chain that supports the displaced persons community in and around America's most diverse zip code. Now settled in Clarkston in her last home, she has created a sense of family for Leon, Frey, Ahmad, and countless others. Today, the organization employs dozens of staff from fifteen different war-torn countries, and the team is just getting started.

As Eleanor Roosevelt's quote affirms on the wall of their Sweet Auburn shop, "It isn't enough to talk about peace. One must believe in it. And it isn't enough to believe in it. One must work at it." Because Kitti insightfully identified the need she was uniquely positioned to meet and then courageously adjusted the course of her life to work at it, her incredible social legacy is still unfolding today.

— REFLECTION —

Where might the unpaved road in your life lead?

Expand your view of the world. Whether it's simply taking a different route home tonight or traveling around the world like Karen and Kym to see something with your own eyes, try stepping outside your comfort zone. Experiencing something outside of our daily routine inevitably changes the way we see the world and can inspire us to take action for those who most need our help.

Yet each of us lives within a personal comfort zone. It can be a helpful exercise to define your own safe space, then consider where and when you might be open to pushing the boundaries to, as Kitti puts it, explore "outside the bubble."

— • —

After reading about the experiences in this chapter, are you thinking about your own unpaved road? In fact, quickly flip back to Chapter Two and skim over those seventeen Sustainable Development Goals again. Did any of them give you pause or startle you with information you hadn't known before?

Perhaps like Harper from Chapter Two, hearing a story like Abdo's will pique your curiosity. Or maybe your comfort zone isn't defined by geography. Kitti's "last house" is located just a few miles away from her former neighborhood, yet it catapulted her outside her social comfort zone. And our family has traveled all over the world, but it was sharing a home with Lotus that put us outside our individual sense of familiarity.

Now, take a moment to reflect on your own comfort zone. How would you define it? Take a look at the graphic below and try to identify which bubble defines your comfort zone. Breaking out of this circle of security and familiarity may define the "unpaved road" for you.

My Unpaved Road

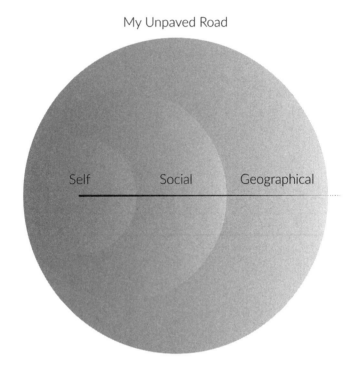

Figure 5.1

Self. You feel in control of your environment, deal with minimum levels of uncertainty, and protect well-established personal boundaries. Your personal space is a hallowed sanctuary, and your time is both precious and priceless. If you relate to this description, you may be cozying up in an individual comfort zone.

Back in Chapter One, Marlene stepped outside her individual bubble when she began giving her cherished forty-three-minute blocks of time to Jeff.

Social. You prefer established social settings where you understand the unspoken rules and derive pleasure in being a member of the community. Folks around you generally come from a similar background and share a foundational language in expressing themselves and the world around them. If this feels familiar, perhaps you have an opportunity to step outside your social sanctum.

I imagine that the first time James from the tent community in Chapter Four shouted at Thomas, the young manager must have been gripped with apprehension, for at least a fleeting moment, before he turned and engaged with the gruff voice.

Geographical. Maybe you have not traveled a whole lot, and foreign places intimidate you. Perhaps the statistics shared in Chapter Two's Reflection gave you a jolt, but the idea of moving outside your geographic comfort zone is unnerving. Some may find the idea of visiting a faraway country to be frightening. Exotic foods, currency exchange, and foreign languages can all feel overwhelming.

> **What kind of party would you never attend?**
>
> *Do the words "black tie" make you shudder? Do you cringe at the idea of attending a rave? What about marching in a Black Lives Matter or LGBTQ protest? How about a conservative Christian church luncheon? Which event do you shrink away from? Maybe you should go check one out.*

> **What if you gave the globe a spin?**
>
> *Quentin from Chapter Three spun the globe as he prepared to leave Afghanistan and return to the States. Perhaps it's not a world globe for you; define a radius that feels stretching to you and give your delineated universe a spin. Then plan to visit that place within the next two years.*

In this chapter, you read about how Kym and Karen were so compelled to help Ukrainian orphans that they mustered up the resolution to overcome a fear of the unknown. It couldn't have been easy for them, and I'm sure they experienced moments of self-doubt and even a yearning to just return home.

Pause here to define your comfort zone. Which bubble are you most interested in bursting?

_____

_____

Is this something you believe is worth doing? If so, consider the following questions.

What fears or insecurities might be holding you back? Is there something you feel drawn to and believe is worth doing, but you're afraid to move forward? Even as I write this book, I am facing my own insecurities. I've never written a book before. But I remain anchored in my belief that sharing my social legacy will benefit others, and it keeps me going. What might be possible if you pushed your own reservations to the side?

Now, flip back to your "unpaved road" bubbles on the previous page. Within your identified bubble, list the comforts you are willing to try to give up. Outside that bubble, outline the fears that may be holding you back. Then, next to each of those fears, jot down a few thoughts on how you will overcome it. Try to be specific.

What might distract you? Karen's first step into uncharted territory involved just one trip to Ukraine; she had designed for herself a limited-time offer, making it easier to not get distracted. What is the time frame you'll allot for yourself and, in that period, how will you fend off distractions to maintain your focus?

THE DEDICATED TIME PERIOD YOU WILL COMMIT TO:

_____

_____

Who's your tribe? Everyone can benefit from a safety net, those people who either walk alongside you or are able to provide confidential, honest, frequent check-ins with you so you never feel alone. Kitti's life partner, Bill, was at her side every step of the way. Our family of three has opened our spare room together, journeying hand in hand. Who are your people?

Detail your tribe:

THOSE WHO WILL WALK THE UNPAVED ROAD WITH YOU:

_____

_____

THOSE WHO WILL HOLD YOU ACCOUNTABLE:

_____

_____

Are you prepared to fail? I will vulnerably confess that I failed Lotus many times. Sometimes I lost my temper with her, a child who only needed unconditional love. Luckily, she was gracious enough to forgive my shortcomings, and I was able to learn from those experiences. So, expect to fall short as you embark on your journey, and don't count it as defeat.

—RESOURCES—

If Lotus's story made an impression on you and if you suspect someone is a victim of trafficking, please contact the National Human Trafficking Hotline toll-free at 1-888-373-7888 or https://humantraffickinghotline.org/training-resources/referral-directory. We can all educate ourselves to be conscientious and informed consumers. You can research where your goods come from and who supplied the labor at https://www.responsiblesourcingtool.org.

If Karen and Kym's story inspired you, get involved with Kym's organization at http://teamworksteam.org. Or, if you prefer staying closer to home, consider hosting a foreign exchange student through your local school system. To see if international adoption might be right for you, check out Adoption.org at https://adoption.org.

If Kitti's story touched you, check out Refuge Coffee at https://www.refugecoffeeco.com. You can get involved in helping with the refugee crisis at https://www.unv.org/become-volunteer. If you speak multiple languages, you can volunteer to provide translation services at https://www.humanrightsfirst.org/asylum/pro-bono-attorneys-and-volunteers. Last but not least, Airbnb and the International Rescue Committee have partnered up to provide refugee housing; if you have a spare room available, visit https://www.airbnb.com/openhomes/refugee-housing.

CHAPTER 6

Living Your Legacy

How your social legacy positions you to live with more intentionality.

> *"To live is the rarest thing in the world.*
> *Most people exist, that is all."*
>
> —OSCAR WILDE

Thank you so much for reading about our family's experiences and coming along this journey with me. Over the previous chapters, I hope you have successfully identified your Offer, that unique contribution that combines your capabilities, passions, personal characteristics, and resources. Alongside that, you should have diagnosed your Offense—that issue or social injustice—that angers you and galvanizes you to action. By fusing your Offer and Offense, you have equipped yourself with a definition of your social legacy, the lasting impact you desire to have on the world around you.

As you pondered your first step and considered whether you were ready to journey outside your comfort zone onto the "unpaved road," you may have narrowed in on an action plan in the past two chapters. Now, I'd like to zoom out and take a broader, panoramic view. What fundamental values underpin your social legacy, and can knowledge of them drive you to live with more specificity and intentionality?

First, write your social legacy here:

_____

_____

Now, peruse the values below and circle those that are most important to you. You may be wondering how many you should circle. Well, enough that in one year or ten years from now, you'll be able to spout them off the top of your head because they're that meaningful and succinct, representing who you are and why you make the choices you make.

VALUES

Achievement/Excellence/Success: In all undertakings, I always put forth my very best effort and do things to the best of my ability. It's important that I accomplish my goals and deliver against targets.

Adventure: I feed on the excitement of new experiences and feel exhilaration in venturing outside my comfort zone.

Altruism: I believe that the well-being of others is as important as my own, and enjoy proactively construing ways to help others.

Authenticity: I am myself in all situations, and I don't teach anything I don't live or believe.

Balance: I cultivate positive energy to foster optimal health and happiness. I am a well-rounded person in pursuit of various interests that contribute to the well-being of myself and those around me.

Beauty: I appreciate and emotionally experience beauty and elegance around me, often pausing to drink in details that others may not see.

Belonging/Affiliation: I reject and will call out any language that minimizes or dehumanizes another person.

Commitment: I think it's extremely important to remain focused and loyal to purposeful goals. I'm driven to live out the things that are important to me.

Community/Harmony: I promote empathy and go out of my way to build trust, choosing to encourage instead of judge. Prioritizing unity and seeking common ground, I recognize and accept people's differences and contributions and can see how they create a greater whole.

Compassion: When confronted with another person's suffering, I feel moved to the point of taking action on his or her behalf.

Competence: I am widely trusted and recognized for effectively and efficiently applying my knowledge and skills to a wide range of circumstances.

Competition/Challenge: Self-driven, I see myself as a bold contender who enjoys overcoming obstacles and who thrives in adversity.

Contribution: I am motivated and feel rewarded by my ability to add value to people, circumstances, and society.

Courage/Confidence: I know myself well and feel good about what I offer to the world. I do not fear mistakes and am brave enough to take on difficult challenges.

Creativity/Expression: I am comfortable with contradictory emotions and ideas, and enjoy arranging them to produce something original and meaningful that represents who I am.

Curiosity/Development/Learning: I seek to learn and grow continually, exploring the world around me to understand where I can make a positive impact. At the end of each day, I pause to reflect and plan for tomorrow.

Dignity: I believe every human deserves and yearns to be seen, heard, and fairly treated. To do my part, I actively listen, observe, and take action to help others feel understood, worthy, and valued.

Diversity: I appreciate and work to recognize, protect, and maintain individual differences. I make an effort to ensure that all people feel valued for their unique perspective and contribution.

Environment: I view our habitat as critical to our well-being, so I mindfully use and maintain resources responsibly, from the way my desk is organized to understanding the impact my actions have on the globe.

Equality/Inclusion: I believe that everyone, without prejudice, has a right to fair treatment. I actively bring in and represent those who are absent.

Excitement: I feel most alive when I'm surrounded by a flurry of activity, people, and events buzzing with energetic commotion as they swirl around me.

Faith/Spirituality: I derive peace and purpose from my beliefs about the meaning of life. They help me understand who I am and connect me to something greater than myself.

Forgiveness: I place a priority on peace and believe that letting go of negative emotions like bitterness and anger leads to freedom, as hurt and resentment are replaced by healing and reconciliation.

Freedom: I value the rights, freedoms, and responsibilities of each human being and our society at large. I keep myself informed and get involved to ensure that my voice is heard and my vote is counted.

Fun/Humor: I enjoy delighting others with lighthearted positivity and make time for fun, because I believe it enables shared joy. It facilitates a sense of camaraderie and reduces stress while maintaining perspective just when we need it most.

Generosity/Charity: I give generously to my family, friends, and those in need. I don't allow resources to go unused or sit idle. And I make life better for others through service and giving.

Grace: I am often described as charming, tactful, or diplomatic, because I walk lightly and try to extend kindness beyond what a person or circumstance might deserve.

Gratitude: I see each day as an unrepeatable miracle, feeling thankful for all I have and content in my circumstances. I journal about my blessings and look for opportunities to share joy and praise.

Health: I seek to live my life fully, exercising wisdom in what I choose to consume with my eyes, mind, and mouth. I develop habits that expand my capabilities and choices in life.

Hope/Optimism: I am naturally upbeat and view circumstances with an open mind. I rarely feel discouraged, and expect the best possible outcome in any given situation.

Independence: I exercise initiative in accomplishing my goals. Rather than waiting for instruction, I take initiative in situations and pursue opportunities.

Innovation: I enjoy challenging the status quo, pushing boundaries to uncover new opportunities for growth and resetting the standard for excellence. I particularly value creativity and originality in problem-solving.

Integrity: Above all, I walk my talk so that my behavior consistently reflects my values. I fight passionately for what I believe in and do the right thing even if it's inconvenient and no one knows I'm doing it.

Justice/Advocacy: I extend myself, sharing power to those without, sharing my voice with those who lack a platform, and defending those who cannot defend themselves.

Knowledge/Expertise: I am blessed with my experience and see it as my responsibility and opportunity to share what

I know with those who can benefit. I make time to teach, mentor, and share my skills and knowledge to make the world a better place.

Leadership: People look to me for direction, because I am able to efficiently sift through complex information, prioritize, communicate, and delegate. I seek to help those around me identify a source of direction in life.

Legacy/Tradition: I believe traditions and rituals give us a chance to commemorate, honor, and pause, providing a positive way to cope with change or sorrow. There is power in rituals, which can build connection, provide closure, offer a sense of identity, and recall emotions even while setting us free from them.

Listening/Understanding: I try to be fully present, listening intently and empathizing with the ideas, concerns, and needs of others. I am known for being attentive, and people feel safe enough to open up and share deeply with me.

Order/Simplicity: I live my life in a disciplined and organized way, which helps me retain focus and channel my energy effectively. I see order and logic as stabilizing forces and take comfort in doing the right things in the right way.

Originality: I try to create and present concepts in new and unexpected ways. And I love it when I discover a fresh perspective that reflects someone's unique, creative, authentic self.

Patriotism: I deeply love my country and will proudly defend its founding principles. I seek out and enjoy camaraderie with others who stand in respect of our nation and pay tribute to those who have dedicated their lives in defending it.

Peace: I pursue a life of calm and lasting harmony. For the world to fell walls and heal divides, I believe it is critical to resolve emotional conflicts and prioritize reconciliation.

Reason: It's important to me that people and society operate with prudence, wisdom, and sound judgment. I respect people who keep themselves informed and exercise fair-mindedness.

Recognition: I often pause to acknowledge those who have done good, worthy work. In particular, I think it's important and motivating to shine a light on unsung heroes.

Responsibility/Stewardship: I think it's fundamentally important to be a dependable person, to honor commitments and deliver on promises. I don't make excuses when things go wrong, and take accountability for my actions.

Security/Safety/Stability: I know my sense of worth and am comfortable with who I am. I believe that all people deserve to feel secure in their basic needs of food and shelter, and that they are entitled to a safe environment, free from abuse.

Service/Support: I am humbled and grateful for all that I have been given, and consider serving others to be a responsibility and a privilege.

Teamwork/Participation: I love working shoulder to shoulder with others, and it's important to me that everyone engages to the best of their ability and exhibits a spirit of cooperation.

Truth: I pursue the most accurate version of history and seek out data that validates and supports its legitimacy. It's very important to me that people are informed on what really happened.

Vision: I hold those who provide a sense of purpose in high regard. I think it's critical for leaders to inspire others with a dream and fuel those around them with the resources and motivation to deliver it.

Wisdom: I place high value on the ability to discern truth, exhibit grace, and take measured action that benefits others. I seek to understand how information and people relate and fit together.

Now, take a moment to review all the values you circled. What do they have in common? Is it clear to you how they underpin your social legacy?

In this last section, you have an opportunity to determine your epitaph. What do you want the people who knew you best to say about you when you're gone? This is an opportunity to integrate your key values into a statement of intentional living.

> *What did you want to be when you were a kid?*
>
> *Who did you envision when you dreamt about becoming an adult one day?*
>
> *That image might help you get started.*

Figure 6.1

Again, I'll share my own example as a thought starter. Back in Chapter Three, I listed my values in my Offer, so they may look familiar. Here's how I assimilated them into my epitaph:

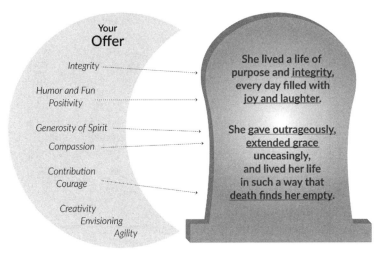

Figure 6.2

You'll notice I didn't incorporate every single value that is important to me, because some may more naturally describe *how* I lived life, not what *kind* of life I lived.

I'd love to see your epitaph and how you have defined your social legacy! Please share them

How will you know you were successful?

Try listing three tangible outcomes with end dates.

Now, set a reminder in your calendar or ask someone in your tribe to prompt you by that date.

at www.social-legacy.com, either publicly on the Community page or privately with me. There, you'll also find photos and other cool stuff from many of the heroes in the stories throughout this book.

As you close this book armed with your social legacy and action plan, I wish you a life of rich meaning and intentionality!

Acknowledgments

I'd like to thank all of the outrageously courageous, passionate, and creative trailblazers who shared their most intimate memories with me over hours of interviews. It has been an absolute honor.

Deepest gratitude to my lifelong mentors, Jim and Vivienne Bechtold, whose honest and generous counsel has shaped me as a wife, mother, and leader. "Home" is brunch in your bright, sunny kitchen. And to the other power couple in our lives, Denise and Dan Ramsey, whose love has wrapped our family in layers of cozy chenille and the spicy comfort of hot cinnamon rolls.

To those who first encouraged me to tell our spare room stories, I am indebted to you. Yarrow Kraner, catalyst of changemakers, the world is better because of you. Sarah Kochling, Nancy Pon, and Mary Rezek, thank you for giving me my first TEDx stage. Your patience as I wrestled with my deepest unexpressed emotions redefines generosity. Paul Smith, you won that dollar years ago and have been inspiring me since. Aubree Curtis, Kobi Yamada, Vanna Novak, and Stacy Katz, you helped me build my earliest framework when I held nothing but an unshaped handful of ideas.

Then, to the marvelous professionals who helped turn concept into reality: Debra Englander, Karen Murgolo, Jane von Mehren, and Heather Jackson, *The Spare Room* would not exist without your patient guidance and steadfast belief. Minki, man of many hats, thank you for the beautifully designed graphics. As always, you took my ideas and made them better.

I am who I am becoming because of those leaders who have believed and invested in me. Profound gratitude and love to Kenneth MacPherson, a real-life superhero to his people; Christy Schrader, a badass who defines feminine strength; Diana Shaheen, who realized my twenty-two-year-old self needed permission to be me; Ravi Chaturvedi, who leads with knowledge and supports with heart; and Tia Jordan, who finds and cultivates the best in everyone.

To those I have had the immense privilege of working alongside and leading, thank you for the fun, partnership, and your grace as I've questioned, endeavored, and evolved. Lisa Xu, for years you thoughtfully enabled me to do what I do at work and at home...感谢心爱的.

Jackie and Jason, we love the McChangs! Evelin, Gail, Alodia, Xiao Xie ayi, and Huang Shu Shu, thank you for pouring into Teo. Steph, Wilson, and friends, thank you for faithfully continuing the monthly birthday parties...so much joy because of you!

Endnotes

Chapter 1

1 The Program for the International Assessment of Adult Competencies (PIAAC) is a large-scale international household study administered in more than forty countries and conducted by the National Center for Education Statistics (NCES) of the U.S. Department of Education. "Adult Literacy in the United States," National Center for Education Statistics, U.S. Department of Education, July 2019, https://nces.ed.gov/datapoints/2019179.asp.

2 "US Literacy Rates by State 2020," World Population Review, accessed September 30, 2020, https://worldpopulationreview.com/states/us-literacy-rates-by-state/.

3 "Adult Literacy Facts," ProLiteracy, accessed September 30, 2020, https://proliteracy.org/Adult-Literacy-Facts.

Chapter 2

1 Anjali Tsui, Dan Nolan, and Chris Amico, "Child Marriage in America: By the Numbers," Frontline, PBS, July 6, 2017, http://apps.frontline.org/child-marriage-by-the-numbers/.

2 Ibid.

3 "Child Marriage—Shocking Statistics," Unchained at Last, accessed September 30, 2020, https://www.unchainedatlast.org/child-marriage-shocking-statistics/.

4 "Statistics of the Year 2018: Winners Announced," Royal Statistical Society, December 18, 2018, https://rss.org.uk/news-publication/news-publications/2018/general-news/statistics-of-the-year-2018-winners-announced/. https://www.statslife.org.uk/news/4026-statistics-of-the-year-2018-winners-announced.

5 Edward Humes, "The US Recycling System Is Garbage," *Sierra*, June 26, 2019, https://www.sierraclub.org/sierra/2019-4-july-august/feature/us-recycling-system-garbage.

6 Erin McCormick et al., "Where Does Your Plastic Go? Global Investigation Reveals America's Dirty Secret," *Guardian*, June 17, 2019, https://www.theguardian.com/us-news/2019/jun/17/recycled-plastic-america-global-crisis.

7 "The Lost Boys of the Sudan," The State of the World's Children 1996, UNICEF, https://www.unicef.org/sowc96/closboys.htm.

8 Laura Smith-Spark and David McKenzie, "UK Withholds Rwanda Aid over Claims It Backs Congo Rebels," CNN, November 30, 2012, https://edition.cnn.com/2012/11/30/world/africa/congo-uk-rwanda-rebels/.

9 Jessica Semega et al., "Income and Poverty in the United States: 2018," United States Census Bureau, September 10, 2019, https://www.census.gov/library/publications/2019/demo/p60-266.html.

10 Mehruba Chowdhury, "The Worst Consequences of Poverty," Borgen Project Blog, Borgen Project, February 28, 2018, https://borgenproject.org/worst-consequences-of-poverty/.

11 Esteban Ortiz-Ospina, "Children and Poverty: Evidence from New World Bank Data," Our World in Data, February 22, 2017, https://ourworldindata.org/children-and-poverty-results-from-new-data.

12 Shelley Callahan, "Understanding Child Poverty: Facts and Statistics," On the Road, Children Incorporated, January 12, 2020, https://childrenincorporated.org/understanding-child-poverty-facts-and-statistics/.

13 Ilze Slabbert, "Domestic Violence and Poverty: Some Women's Experiences," *Research on Social Work Practice* 27, no. 2 (March 2017): 223–230, https://doi.org/10.1177/1049731516662321.

14 "Facts about Poverty and Hunger in America," Feeding America, accessed September 30, 2020, https://www.feedingamerica.org/hunger-in-america/facts.

15 "School Breakfast," No Kid Hungry, accessed September 30, 2020, https://www.nokidhungry.org/what-we-do/school-breakfast.

16 "Over 820 Million People Suffering from Hunger; New UN Report Reveals Stubborn Realities of 'Immense' Global Challenge," UN News, July 15, 2019, https://news.un.org/en/story/2019/07/1042411.

17 World Health Organization, "World Hunger Is Still Not Going Down after Three Years and Obesity Is Still Growing—UN Report," news release, July 15, 2019, https://www.who.int/news-room/detail/15-07-2019-world-hunger-is-still-not-going-down-after-three-years-and-obesity-is-still-growing-un-report.

18 "America's Drug Overdose Epidemic: Putting Data to Action," National Center for Injury Prevention and Control, Centers for Disease Control and Prevention, August 28, 2020, https://www.cdc.gov/injury/features/prescription-drug-overdose/index.html.

19 "Elder Abuse Facts," National Council on Aging, accessed September 30, 2020, https://www.ncoa.org/public-policy-action/elder-justice/elder-abuse-facts/.

20 "Elder Abuse," World Health Organization, June 15, 2020, https://www.who.int/news-room/fact-sheets/detail/elder-abuse.

21 Margaret E. Kruk et al., "Mortality Due to Low-Quality Health Systems in the Universal Health Coverage Era: A Systematic Analysis of Amenable Deaths in 137 Countries," *The Lancet* 392, no. 10160 (November 2018): 2203–2212, https://doi.org/10.1016/S0140-6736(18)31668-4.

22 "Adult Literacy in the United States."

23 "Adult Literacy Facts."

24 "Data for the Sustainable Development Goals," UNESCO Institute of Statistics, accessed September 30, 2020, http://uis.unesco.org.

25 "Trafficking and Slavery Fact Sheet," Free the Slaves, accessed September 30, 2020, https://www.freetheslaves.net/wp-content/uploads/2018/04/Trafficking-ans-Slavery-Fact-Sheet-April-2018.pdf.

26 Heather J. Clawson et al., "Human Trafficking into and within the United States: A Review of the Literature," Office of the Assistant Secretary for Planning and Evaluation, U.S. Department of Health and Human Services, August 30, 2009, https://aspe.hhs.gov/report/human-trafficking-and-within-united-states-review-literature#Trafficking.

27 "Child Marriage around the World," infographic, UNICEF, March 11, 2020, https://www.unicef.org/stories/child-marriage-around-world.

28 "International Day of Zero Tolerance for Female Genital Mutilation, 6 February," United Nations, accessed September 30, 2020, https://www.un.org/en/observances/female-genital-mutilation-day.

29 World Health Organization, "1 in 3 People Globally Do Not Have Access to Safe Drinking Water—UNICEF, WHO," news release, June 18, 2019, https://www.who.int/news-room/detail/18-06-2019-1-in-3-people-globally-do-not-have-access-to-safe-drinking-water-unicef-who.

30 "Freshwater Ecosystems," Conservation International, accessed September 30, 2020, https://www.conservation.org/priorities/fresh-water.

31 "Clean" is defined as not releasing greenhouse gasses or other harmful emissions.

32 Neel Tamhane, "Can Emerging Economies Leapfrog the Energy Transition?" World Economic Forum Annual Meeting, World Economic Forum, January 7, 2020, https://www.weforum.org/agenda/2020/01/can-emerging-economies-leapfrog-the-energy-transition/.

33 "PINC-05. Work Experience—People 15 Years Old and over, by Total Money Earnings, Age, Race, Hispanic Origin, Sex, and Disability Status," United States Census Bureau, accessed September 30, 2020, https://www.census.gov/data/tables/time-series/demo/income-poverty/cps-pinc/pinc-05.html.

34 "Global Estimates of Child Labour: Results and Trends, 2012–2016," International Labour Organization, 2017, https://www.ilo.org/wcmsp5/

groups/public/---dgreports/---dcomm/documents/publication/
wcms_575499.pdf.

35 Defined as residing within five hundred meters' walking distance to a bus
stop or low-capacity transport system, or within one thousand meters of a
railway and/or ferry terminal.

36 "Internet Usage Statistics: The Internet Big Picture," Internet World Stats,
accessed September 30, 2020, https://www.internetworldstats.com/stats.
htm.

37 "The Mobile Gender Gap Report 2020," GSMA Connected Women, GSM
Association, 2020, https://www.gsma.com/r/gender-gap/.

38 "Dünya genelinde öksüz ve yetim çocukların sayısı 140 milyon," Anadolu
Agency, June 4, 2017, https://www.aa.com.tr/tr/dunya/dunya-genelinde
-oksuz-ve-yetim-cocuklarin-sayisi-140-milyon/790353.

39 "Fact Sheets," Congressional Coalition on Adoption Institute, http://www.
ccainstitute.org/resources/fact-sheets.

40 "Disability Inclusion," World Bank Group, May 15, 2020, https://www.
worldbank.org/en/topic/disability.

41 "Disability Statistics: Information, Charts, Graphs and Tables," Disabled
World, March 30, 2020, https://www.disabled-world.com/disability/
statistics/.

42 "Goal 11: Make Cities Inclusive, Safe, Resilient and Sustainable," Sustainable Development Goals, United Nations, accessed September 30, 2020,
https://www.un.org/sustainabledevelopment/cities/.

43 "The State of Homelessness in America," Council of Economic Advisers,
September 2019, https://www.whitehouse.gov/wp-content/uploads/2019
/09/The-State-of-Homelessness-in-America.pdf.

44 "Minimum Wage," U.S. Department of Labor, accessed September 30,
2020, https://www.dol.gov/general/topic/wages/minimumwage.

45 "Food Waste Facts," OzHarvest, accessed September 30, 2020, https://
www.ozharvest.org/what-we-do/environment-facts/.

46 "Fighting Peak Phosphorus," Massachusetts Institute of Technology,
accessed September 30, 2020, https://web.mit.edu/12.000/www/m2016
/finalwebsite/solutions/phosphorus.html.

47 Mette Bendixen et al., "Time Is Running Out for Sand," July 2, 2019,
Nature, https://www.nature.com/articles/d41586-019-02042-4.

48 "Goal 13: Take Urgent Action to Combat Climate Change and Its Impacts,"
Sustainable Development Goals, United Nations, accessed September 30,
2020, https://www.un.org/sustainabledevelopment/climate-change/.

49 David Wallace-Wells, "The Uninhabitable Earth," Intelligencer, *New York
Magazine*, accessed September 30, 2020, https://nymag.com/intelli-
gencer/2017/07/climate-change-earth-too-hot-for-humans.html.

50 "Goal 14: Conserve and Sustainably Use the Oceans, Seas and Marine Resources," Sustainable Development Goals, United Nations, accessed September 30, 2020, https://www.un.org/sustainabledevelopment/oceans/.

51 "The Largest Cleanup in History," Ocean Cleanup, accessed September 30, 2020, https://theoceancleanup.com.

52 "The Great Pacific Garbage Patch," Ocean Cleanup, accessed September 30, 2020, https://theoceancleanup.com/great-pacific-garbage-patch/.

53 "Sustainably Manage Forests, Combat Desertification, Halt and Reverse Land Degradation, Halt Biodiversity Loss," Sustainable Development Goals, United Nations, accessed September 30, 2020, https://www.un.org/sustainabledevelopment/biodiversity/.

54 Ingrid Schulte et al., "Protecting and Restoring Forests: A Story of Large Commitments yet Limited Progress," New York Declaration on Forests Five-Year Assessment Report, NYDF Assessment Partners, September 2019, https://forestdeclaration.org/images/uploads/resource/2019NYDFReport.pdf.

55 "Deforestation and Forest Degradation: Overview," World Wildlife Fund, accessed September 30, 2020, https://www.worldwildlife.org/threats/deforestation-and-forest-degradation.

56 "UN Report: Nature's Dangerous Decline 'Unprecedented'; Species Extinction Rates 'Accelerating,'" Sustainable Development Goals, United Nations, May 6, 2019, https://www.un.org/sustainabledevelopment/blog/2019/05/nature-decline-unprecedented-report/.

57 Christine Dell'Amore, "Species Extinction Happening 1,000 Times Faster Because of Humans?" National Geographic, May 30, 2014, https://www.nationalgeographic.com/news/2014/5/140529-conservation-science-animals-species-endangered-extinction/.

58 "Pet Statistics," ASPCA, accessed September 30, 2020, https://www.aspca.org/animal-homelessness/shelter-intake-and-surrender/pet-statistics.

59 "Universal Declaration of Human Rights," United Nations, accessed September 30, 2020, https://www.un.org/en/universal-declaration-human-rights/#:~:text=All%20human%20beings%20are%20born,in%20a%20spirit%20of%20brotherhood.

60 "OHCHR and NHRIs," Office of the United Nations High Commissioner for Human Rights, accessed September 30, 2020, https://www.ohchr.org/EN/Countries/NHRI/Pages/NHRIMain.aspx.

61 "Police Violence Map," Mapping Police Violence, accessed September 30, 2020, https://mappingpoliceviolence.org.

62 "Safety Net: Cyberbullying's Impact on Young People's Mental Health," Children's Society and YoungMinds, accessed September 30, 2020,

https://www.childrenssociety.org.uk/sites/default/files/social-media-cyberbullying-inquiry-full-report_0.pdf.

63 "Bullying Statistics," PACER's National Bullying Prevention Center, May 2020, https://www.pacer.org/bullying/resources/stats.asp.

64 "51 Critical Cyberbullying Statistics in 2020," BroadbandSearch.net, accessed September 30, 2020, https://www.broadbandsearch.net/blog/cyber-bullying-statistics.

65 "Figures at a Glance," UNHCR Philippines, accessed September 30, 2020, https://www.unhcr.org/ph/figures-at-a-glance.

66 "Reality Check: Migrant Workers Rights with Four Years to the Qatar 2022 World Cup," Amnesty International, accessed September 30, 2020, https://www.amnesty.org/en/latest/campaigns/2019/02/reality-check-migrant-workers-rights-with-four-years-to-qatar-2022-world-cup/.

67 Daniel Costa and Philip Martin, "Coronavirus and Farmworkers: Farm Employment, Safety Issues, and the H-2A Guestworker Program," Economic Policy Institute, March 24, 2020, https://www.epi.org/publication/coronavirus-and-farmworkers-h-2a/.

68 Zoe Willingham and Silva Mathema, "Protecting Farmworkers from Coronavirus and Securing the Food Supply," Center for American Progress, April 23, 2020, https://www.americanprogress.org/issues/economy/reports/2020/04/23/483488/protecting-farmworkers-coronavirus-securing-food-supply/.

Chapter 3

1 "Police Begin Probe of 'Fake Landlord' Who Disappeared," Shanghai Municipal People's Government, January 12, 2012, http://www.shanghai.gov.cn/shanghai/node27118/node27818/u22ai66074.html.

2 Jeff Tavss, "3 South Florida Cities Ranked among Most Dangerous in U.S.," WPLG Local 10, March 2, 2018, https://www.local10.com/news/2018/03/02/3-south-florida-cities-ranked-among-most-dangerous-in-us/.

Chapter 4

1 "Hydrocephalus Fact Sheet," Office of Communications and Public Liaison, National Institute of Neurological Disorders and Stroke, National Institutes of Health, April 2020, https://www.ninds.nih.gov/disorders/patient-caregiver-education/fact-sheets/hydrocephalus-fact-sheet.

2 Lola E. Peters, "Seattle Is Addicted to Bad Narratives about Homelessness," Crosscut, September 2, 2019, https://crosscut.com/2019/09/seattle-addicted-bad-narratives-about-homelessness.

Chapter 5

1 "About," Clarkston Community Center, March 2, 2018, https://clarkston-communitycenter.org/about-us.

2 "About," City of Clarkston, accessed September 30, 2020, https://www.clarkstonga.gov/about.

About the Author

Photo by Minki Chang

Emily Chang is currently the CEO for McCann Worldgroup, China, and previously served as the Chief Marketing Officer for Starbucks, China, and the Chief Commercial Officer for InterContinental Hotels group, Greater China. Earlier in her career, she led Retail Marketing for Apple in Asia-Pacific and began her career with eleven years at Procter & Gamble. She is an action-oriented visionary known for cross-cultural team engagement, innovative brand building, and authentic people leadership.

Emily has spoken at select conferences and events, including Fortune Most Powerful Women's Summit, C2 in Montréal, and has delivered three TEDx talks. With her husband of twenty years, eleven-year-old daughter, rescue mutt named Holly Berry, and pygmy hedgehog named Scarlett Jellybean, she has shared her spare room with sixteen young people, five dogs, one turtle, one guinea pig, and 129 snails. To learn more about Emily, please visit www. social-legacy.com.